AN UNDIVIDED
Love

AN UNDIVIDED

LOVING AND LIVING FOR CHRIST

ADOLPHE MONOD

CONSTANCE K. WALKER
EDITOR AND TRANSLATOR

SOLID GROUND
CHRISTIAN BOOKS
P.O. BOX 660132 • VESTAVIA HILLS • ALABAMA 35266

© 2009 by Constance K. Walker

All rights reserved. No part of this book may be reproduced, stored in a retrieval system, or transmitted in any form or by any means—electronic, mechanical, photocopy, recording, or otherwise—except for brief quotations for the purpose of review or comment, without the prior permission of the publisher, Solid Ground Christian Books, P.O. Box 660132, Vestavia Hills, Alabama 35266.

Unless otherwise indicated, all Scripture quotations are taken from The Holy Bible, English Standard Version, copyright © 2001 by Crossway Bibles, a division of Good News Publishers. Used by permission. All rights reserved

Scripture quotations marked KJV are taken from the Authorized (King James) Version of the Holy Bible.

Cover image courtesy of Ken Jenkins
[For other examples of his work, please visit www.kenjenkins.com]

Cover design by Borgo Design

Printed in the United States of America

978-159925-211-7

TRANSLATOR'S DEDICATION

*For Mom and Dad,
whose unfailing love and encouragement
prepared me to accept the love of my heavenly Father;*

*and for Bill,
who first introduced me to Jesus
and who has been my delightful partner along faith's pilgrimage.*

Contents

Biographical Sketch   9
Translator's Preface   11

✂ *part one* COME AND DRINK 15

    1 Give Me Your Heart   19
    2 Are You Thirsty?   41

✂ *part two* BEHOLD YOUR GOD 71

    3 God Is Love   75
    4 I am the Resurrection and the Life   107
    5 Too Late! (God Faithful in His Threats)   129

✂ *part three* TRUST IN THE LORD 151

    6 Embracing God's Plan   155
    7 The Happiness of the Christian Life   177

Adolphe Monod, circa 1855

Biographical Sketch

Adolphe Monod (1802-1856) was from a family prominent in the French Reformed Church. Though descended from a line of protestant ministers, he struggled for many years before coming to a personal faith in Christ. As a young man, he joined the pastoral staff of the Reformed Church in Lyon, where his strong gospel-centered preaching soon drew opposition and led to his dismissal. Staying on in Lyon, he founded a rapidly growing independent evangelical congregation. He then spent a decade as a professor at the seminary in Montauban and another decade at the Reformed Church in Paris. The vibrant clarity and warmth of his preaching made him a leader in the evangelical church of his day, with his sermons and books widely published during his lifetime.

Those facts, however, fail to capture the spirit of the man. His was a strong and passionate faith, in part because of his early spiritual struggles. He was also a man of deep integrity, a keen mind, and a caring, pastoral heart. All of these qualities were augmented and set off by his natural gift for speaking. Yet even as his renown grew, Adolphe Monod remained a truly humble man. A week before his death he said "I have a Savior! He has freely saved me through his shed blood, and I want it to be known that I lean uniquely on that poured out blood. All my righteous acts, all my works which have been praised, all my preaching that has been appreciated and sought after—all that is in my eyes only filthy rags."

Translator's Preface

A listener recalls, "I was then twelve to fifteen years old, an age when one can scarcely listen to a discourse, much less a sermon, without impatience to see it end. Those of Adolphe Monod always lasted more than an hour and sometimes an hour and a half, yet they never seemed long to me. They made such a deep, lively impression on me that I can still hear the fine resonant timbre of his voice, and in reading his printed sermons, I note minor changes in sentences that I still recall in their entirety." [1]

With testimonies such as that, it is no wonder Adolphe Monod has been called "the voice of the Awakening." Those who came out of curiosity to hear the preaching of a celebrated orator would often leave the service pierced to the heart by his message, while the mature Christians in his congregations came back again and again to be transported by his preaching into the very presence of God and to have their faith stretched and challenged. Monod was probably the most articulate, engaging, and powerful spokesman for the evangelical movement that first swept across France and Switzerland in the 1820's. Others, including Aldophe's older brother, Frédéric, were more influential as leaders of the movement, but none could expound its doctrine—the central

---

[1] Paul Stapfer, *Bossuet et Adolphe Monod*, Paris, 1898, p 182, quoted by Marc Boegner in *Adolphe Monod, Prédicateur de l'Église Réformée*, Paris, Éditions Berger-Levrault, 1956, p 21.

core of its faith—quite as clearly or persuasively or appealingly as Adolphe Monod.

What was it that made Monod's preaching so effective? One component was certainly his oratorical skills. From all reports his voice had a remarkable dynamic range and a pleasing tone, and he was a naturally gifted speaker. Yet these qualities were merely the vehicle for conveying the message. It was the clarity of his thought and intellect that made the message cogent, it was the strength of his faith and character that made it persuasive, it was the sincerity of his concern for the souls of others that made it attractive, and it was the depth of his love for God that made it vibrant. For all his renown, Monod was a truly humble man, deeply and passionately devoted to his Savior and tirelessly committed to making the treasures of the gospel known.

Monod's published sermons, essays, and books were popular during his lifetime, but to modern readers he is best known for his *Farewells* (or *Les Adieux*). This series of short informal teachings, given to friends and family over the last six months of his life, encapsulate his spiritual legacy. A new edition was recently published under the title *Living in the Hope of Glory*.[2] The present volume shows Monod in a more typical setting. Here you will find the same warmth of soul, the same firmness of doctrine, the same sincere heart of love for God that mark his farewells, but you will also find a more thorough and extended development of his themes.

An Undivided Love exemplifies Monod's exposition of the essence of the evangelical faith in his day as in ours. Part One deals with establishing, growing and maintaining the kind of personal heart-relationship with God that transforms a life and gives it an eternal perspective. Part Two shows us something of the nature of our God, nourishing our love for him as we are led to understand his deep abiding love for us,

---

[2] P&R Publishing, Phillipsburg NJ, 2002. This volume also contains a brief biography of Adolphe Monod.

his fatherly discipline, and his sovereign victory over death. Finally, Part Three describes how our faith will change the way we live, strengthening us to trust God and cling to him even in difficult or perplexing circumstances, and guiding us into abiding joy and peace as we submit to him and to his Word. In the introductions to the three parts of the book, I attempt to relate these themes to my own faith pilgrimage.

In translating and editing material from another language and time, one is treading a fine line between history and clarity. Here, as in *Living in the Hope of Glory*, an effort has been made to preserve as much as possible of Monod's gracious style and phraseology, while still making his message flow naturally to a modern reader. The sermons have been translated from nineteenth century French editions.[3] Quite long by modern standards, they have been shortened slightly by making deletions in peripheral material. Footnotes from the original published sermons are marked with Monod's initials "[A.M.]." All others have been supplied by the editor/translator. The chapters have been broken into sections to guide the reader.

It is a daunting task to translate the words of a celebrated orator of another era. In this endeavor, as with *Living in the Hope of Glory*, I have relied on much prayer as well as the help and support of others. I particularly want to acknowledge:

—My husband, Bill, whose unfailing patience, encouragement, and understanding have made my task so much easier;

—William Edgar, friend, brother, and fellow-disciple of Adolphe Monod, whose confidence in my abilities gave me courage to begin, and who has once again graciously served as my linguistic consultant;

---

[3] Six of the seven sermons were taken from *Sermons, Deuxième Édition* (Vol. 1-4), Paris, Librarie de Ch. Meyrueis et Comp., 1855-1860. *I Am the Resurrection and the Life* was first published for the 100th anniversary of Monod's birth in *Sermons Choisis, Édition du Centenaire*, Paris, Librairie Fischbacher, 1902, which served as my source.

—Sarah G. Byrd, precious friend, kindred spirit, and writer of Christian fantasy for young people, who has lovingly pointed out awkward or unclear constructions and kept my infinitives firmly united, while offering much encouraging praise;

—Linda Purnell and the staff of Duke University's Inter-Library Loan office, who cheerfully persevered in the challenge of obtaining a complete and consistent nineteenth century set of Monod's sermons long after I was ready to give up;

—Michael Gaydosh at Solid Ground Christian Books, whose love for Adolphe Monod, zeal for this project, and professional know-how have made him a joy to work with; and

—Ken Jenkins, master photographer, who graciously allowed us to use "Morning at Greenbrier" as our cover image.

Though Scripture itself should certainly be the primary focus of our reading, there is great profit to be gained from considering the words of giants of the faith whose teachings have stood the test of time. May you discover, as you read and ponder these pages, a fresh perspective on the Biblical faith that unites us, and may your Christian walk be enriched.

Constance K. Walker
Durham, North Carolina

part one
COME AND DRINK

(John 6:35)

part one

At first, there seemed every hope of finding real satisfaction in life. All the world's promises were out there. "Maintain health, get a good education, embark on a rewarding career, enjoy marriage and family, perhaps take up a hobby; and you will be content." But as one goal after another was attained without bringing the promised fulfillment, a sense of restlessness and frustration began to mount. Some key element of my life was missing, but what was it?

Then on August 11, 1975 I found the answer to my longings—or rather, it found me! I had become willing to consider the possibility that Christianity might have something to offer, and I was reading John's Gospel. As I reached the fourth chapter, I was overwhelmed by a sense of Christ's presence. He knew all about the Samaritan woman's life, and he knew all about mine. Jesus saw it all, knew it all, and—astoundingly—loved me anyhow!

God's loving desire for our hearts, his unique ability to be all that those hearts require, and the amazing sacrifice he was willing to pay to gain them are the subject of the first sermon. "Give Me Your Heart" expresses in flowing, powerful, persuasive language the essence of the gospel in Monod's day and in ours. Though outwardly addressed to those who have not yet yielded their hearts to God, it will rekindle the love of those of us who have been walking many years with our Lord, and it will challenge us to be sure that our hearts are still fully given to him.

Yes, Jesus was the key missing element in my life—I have never doubted that—but giving him my heart did not put an end to all my longings. In fact, the closer we get to God, the closer we want to get. Our hearts thirst for fuller, more intimate fellowship with him, for more perfect holiness, for relief from suffering. In the second sermon, "Are You Thirsty?" Monod shows us how to put these longings in an eternal perspective and find satisfaction in this life, even as we await full, unhindered, and unbroken communion with God in eternity. Then he challenges us to look beyond ourselves, reaching out to help satisfy the thirst of others by leading them to the Savior.

—*CKW*

GIVE ME YOUR HEART

(Paris, 1850)

Proverbs 23:26

My son, give me your heart.

A HEART TO GIVE

There has been no shortage of definitions for human nature. There is no philosophy that hasn't attempted its own, but is man any better known? The Bible, the most practical of books and the least systematic, takes the opposite approach. Instead of defining man without revealing him, it reveals him without defining him. Here in my text, he is depicted indirectly and almost by chance through a single trait, but a trait that brings light to the very root of the matter, a trait that you will easily recognize. Man is a creature who has a heart to give

THE NATURE OF MAN'S HEART

The center of man is the moral man, and the center of moral man is his heart. Here, by the heart I do not mean tender affections, still less emotional demonstrations. I take the word in its more masculine and more serious sense, which includes all types of personalities, all ages, and all degrees of culture. The heart, for me, is the seat of the emotions, conscience, and love—all of which belong to that inner region that is the primitive and substantive soil of human nature.

Intelligence and logic, with their admirable clarity, penetrate less deeply. Indeed, there is less of a man in the intellect that makes profound critiques of a sacred text or a book of canon than there is in the faith of the heart that launches itself out into the midst of the void with only a "word" coming "from the mouth of God" (Matthew 4:4) as its support. There is less of a man in the logic that discusses the relationship of man to God and of God to man than there is in the repentance of the heart that says to God, "Against you, you only, have I sinned" (Psalm 51:4), or in the needs of the heart that cries out to him, "My soul thirsts for you . . . in a dry and weary land" (Psalm 63:1).

But this heart that is within us and, more than anything else, *is* us is also a heart that aspires to give itself. Beyond that, it finds itself only in giving itself away. To be loved is its joy, but to love is its life. It is in our hearts that the full truth of the Lord's word, "It is more blessed to give than to receive" (Acts 20:35), finds its application. Or rather, for the heart, to give is to receive; to give freely is to receive abundantly; and in order to fully possess itself, it must give itself without reservation. Lacking this natural nourishment, our heart folds in on us—or rather against us. Turning to egotism, it gnaws its way through the bosom that contains it without satisfying itself. Given away it would bear us up, but kept it weighs us down. Given away it would cause us to live, but kept it kills us. There is no one who doesn't seek a place of rest for his heart.

Competing Claims for Our Hearts

God answers the heart engaged in that search with the words of my text, saying, "to me." This response is even more sensitive and tender in a completely literal translation: "Give, my son, your heart to me." Alas, that *to me* is neither the only one that the heart has heard, nor the first to which it may have listened.

"To me," says sin with its covetousness, and many hearts have thrown themselves into that wide open pathway until a belated experience taught them that sin only scratches the heart's needs in order to irritate them and that the most alluring seduction is followed by the bitterest aftertaste. Isn't that true?

"To me," says the world with its pomp and pleasures, and too many other hearts have been captured by that bait until they have recognized that the world, even the innocent world—if it ever was—has nothing to fill the heart's void except its own void, which adds itself to the other instead of filling it. Isn't that true?

"To me," says natural affection in the form of a mother, a spouse, or a child, and how many hearts have given themselves without qualms to an inclination that seemed to have the cry of nature and even the approval of God, until they found that there is no creature in the world who can give rest to another creature? Alas, even if he could give it to him, what kind of rest would that be, reduced to reckon day by day with possible accidents, probable illness, and certain death? Isn't that true?

Then it is that God comes. Or rather, since he was the first to come but without gaining access, we should say that God mercifully comes back, after all the others. He is content to take that humble place provided that he is welcomed in the end, even as a last resort, and he says to us, "My son, give your heart to me."

Who Is This God?

God, I say, but what God? Strange question, but all too necessary today when this sacred name is turned to such diverse uses—even to such profane uses.

God of the Trinity

The God who asks for your heart is the God who reveals himself in Scripture; the God of Jesus Christ; God the Father, Son, and Holy Spirit. Do not treat that doctrine as theological speculation. It is a mystery. More than that, it is "*the* mystery," but a mystery full "of godliness" (1 Timothy 3:16). There is the Father, who has loved us so much that he would strike his only Son in order to spare us, while hating sin so much that he could not spare us except by striking his only Son. There is the Son, who caused all the fullness of the Deity to dwell in our midst, clothed in a mortal body in which he also bore our sins on the tree. There is the Holy Spirit, who, coming to dwell within us, makes us one with the Son as he is one with the Father (John 17:22), and who makes us participants in the divine nature (2 Peter 1:4).

The fact that it is this very God who speaks to you in my text is made apparent enough simply by the name that he gives you there: my son. That name has its truth only in the mouth of this God who is thrice holy and thrice good. As poor fallen and rebellious creatures, we are sons only because the Father has adopted us in his beloved son (Ephesians 1:5-6). We are sons only because the Son "is not ashamed to call [us] brothers" (Hebrews 2:11). We are sons only because the Holy Spirit has sealed us with the Father's seal and instructed us to cry out, "Abba! Father!" (Romans 8:15).

There, there is the God, the only God who asks for our heart. He is the personal God. Better yet, we say with Scripture that he is "the living and true God" (1 Thessalonians 1:9), the God who wants to maintain a warm, personal relationship with us, because he has a heart that responds to ours and that seeks ours (see e.g. Judges 10:16, 1 Samuel 13:14). He is God made man, whom we can love as truly and as naturally as we love a brother or a friend, and yet, through a marvelous union, he is also the spiritual God who enters into an inner communion with us that we cannot know or conceive of with any created being.

The Only God Who Cares

Your heart! What other God is there who cares about it? It is not the God of Pharisaism, who is amply and abundantly satisfied if your body is zealous for his worship. He is happy if your knee is bent down to the ground, if your flesh is emaciated by fasting, if your mouth has pronounced a few rote prayers, or if your hand extends itself in meritorious alms.

It is not the God of Pantheism, who blends in turn with the human spirit or with inanimate nature, and who can have no personal feelings, since he has no self-existence. For him giving and receiving, loving and being loved, creating and being created are all the same. Beyond that, truth and falsehood, good and evil, being or not being are all blurred together; or rather they lose themselves in a universal negation that is adorned with the superb name of absolute unity.

It is not the God of Deism, who gives life without giving himself and who creates in order to unburden himself. This God is distant from his creatures, lost from sight—and from life—and is locked in the frigid ice of a fatherless creation and an uncaring providence. He makes existence an eternal winter and the world an icy tomb of which he himself is only the statue.[1]

I have said nothing of the God of Islam, who repays a bloodthirsty and fatalistic devotion with the impure currency of a self-centered and carnal pleasure. Nor have I mentioned

---

[1] This perhaps refers to the statue of the one buried in the tomb.

the God of Paganism—I should have said its thousand gods—who gives back to man with interest the lessons of impiety and injustice that they receive from him. Nor have I spoken of the many other gods that man has created and created in his own image.

Thus, outside of Jesus Christ (Jesus Christ already come or still awaited, it matters little; the spirit who inspires a Saint Paul is also the one who inspires a Solomon or a David), no religion offers anything that resembles the invitation of my text: "My son, give me your heart." Give me your observances, says the God of the Pharisees. Give me your personality, says the God of Hegel. Give me your intellect, says the God of Kant. Give me your sword, says the God of Mohammed. Give me your lust, says the God of Homer or Virgil. It remains for the God of Jesus Christ to say, "Give me your heart."

A Heart Relationship

God takes up this contrast with all the others gods[2] and makes it the essence and the glory of his doctrine. For him, giving one's heart to God—that "heart" from which "flow the springs of life" (Proverbs 4:23)—is not just an obligation of godliness, it is its very foundation; it is its beginning, its middle, and its end; it is the unmistakable mark of a true conversion. You tell me that a man has believed in the gospel of grace. That's good, but has he believed with a living faith? You tell me that he has made an irreproachable profession, but is that profession sincere? You tell me that his conduct is always exemplary before his peers, but is that conduct holy before God? You tell me that he is at the forefront of Christian works, but does he bring a Christian spirit to them?

---

[2] Literally "this rejection by [or of] all the other gods." This seems to be a reference to the observation that all the other gods reject our hearts while he alone desires them.

But tell me that he has given his heart to God, and all other questions are superfluous. Faith, works, grace, holiness, a new creation—it is all there.

Very well, you who don't have this totality of the gospel and who sense within you that you lack it (for I want you alone to be the judge of that), it is a matter of knowing today whether you want finally to lay hold of it. You who hear God in my text, place yourself without distraction before the practical question that it raises and tell me whether you want to give your heart to the God of Jesus Christ.

Our Heart's Resting Place

"My son, give your heart to me;" to me in whom alone your heart can rest and for whom it yearns without knowing it.

Your heart has been kept from giving itself fully to any created being, because none of them has all that it requires. Yet, your heart will find all it needs in the God of Jesus Christ, and without him those needs will never be met. More than that, without him your heart will never really understand its needs, for this living God both satisfies them and reveals them to us at the same time.

Among all created beings, take the one you know to be most loveable and most loved. Isn't it true that you cannot try to yield yourself to his love without soon finding a barrier that unmercifully stops the impulse of your heart; a barrier that seems to say to you with bitter defiance, "You will come this far and no farther"?

We Need the Eternal

Why is that? It is because the creature is mortal. There is not a day when you have no reason to say to yourself in the morning, "He could be taken away from me before evening."

But suppose you could give your heart to an object from whom nothing in the world could separate you and to whom you were permitted to yield yourself with the joy of life, the freshness of life, the certainty of life, and the immortal power of life! Very well, this God whom I proclaim to you is what your heart requires. He "is the same yesterday and today and forever" (Hebrews 13:8). Hold fast to him; he will in no wise escape from you. Call to him; he will always answer. Count on him; he will never fail you. And when you yourself "depart and are no more" (see Psalm 39:13), it will be to go elsewhere in order to behold him without a veil and to unite yourself to him without hindrance.

We Need the Infinite

Why else would you find this barrier to a full giving of your heart to a created being? It is because that creature, even if he were immortal, is finite. How could he respond to the infinite needs of your heart? Enclosed within the narrow confines of the flesh, constrained by his will, limited by his illumination, equally incapable of testifying to all that he feels and of sensing all that your heart expects from his, how could he be enough for you? Perhaps in an impulsive moment, touched by so much devotion, so many attractions, such varied worthy traits, you think that there is nothing more to desire in your happiness except to see it continue. But the very next moment, you return to yourself and step out of your tender illusions. In spite of your best efforts to contain it, this cry escapes from you: "And yet, that really isn't it. My heart is begging for something else!"

Very well, that something else, that infinite thing that will fill, that will overflow the full capacity of your heart, you will find in the God whom I proclaim to you. You will find it in this God who possesses light and power and truth and life, all without measure. No, he himself *is* all of that, and it is from his bosom that everything on earth that has some share in those sacred names flows forth like an inexhaustible treasure.

Light, power, truth, and life are scattered fragments of "the one who is" (see Exodus 3:14), leading you to God, like so many divergent streams leading to their common source. In attaching yourself to him, you will gather together the infinite variety of all these gifts in an unchangeable unity.

WE NEED THE HOLY

Finally, why do we find this barrier to giving our hearts fully to another creature? It is because that creature is sinful and, if he knows himself at all, reduced to joining you in saying, "I know that nothing good dwells in me" (Romans 7:18). And you could abandon yourself to him without reservation? What! That fallen creature for whom you need to beg for God's forgiveness as you do for yourself; that creature in whom you find the same battle of the Spirit against the flesh that takes place in you; that creature whose infirmities and weaknesses you must bear with each day, just as he must bear with them in you—is that the one in whom you should seek and in whom you could find what your heart demands? Oh, unworthy thought!

Give fresh air to that unhappy soul who struggles in an atmosphere unable to sustain life. Give daylight to that prisoner who groans in a deep dungeon far from the sweet gleam of the sun. Give bread to the hungry, water to the thirsty—and give to man's heart, as the object of his supreme attachment, a being who is "holy, innocent, unstained, separated from sinners" (Hebrews 7:26). Love for such a being can, at last, be the holiness of our hearts, and serving him the holiness of our lives! Very well, in these traits, how can you fail to recognize the God I proclaim to you?

WE NEED THE GOD OF JESUS CHRIST

Yes, my brother, give, give your heart to the God of Jesus Christ. This eternal God, this infinite God, this holy God is the only one made for your heart, and your heart is made for him alone.³ He is the one your heart cried out for before knowing him, and how much more will it cry out for him once it has begun to know him? If you have merely glimpsed him, you will henceforth find your rest only in him. The heart of man is made in such a way—thanks be to the one who formed it!—that it cannot leave its attachment anywhere, if it conceives of the possibility of carrying it higher. Though you may well have climbed the ladder of creatures, moving always to those more worthy, something will always urge you to climb higher. As long as there is a God in the universe, nothing less will be able to satisfy your heart. Him or no one! Him or a frightful void and a bitter disgust!

I will go further. Him for the joy of your heart or him for its torment! His love can allow you no rest apart from him. Your drunkenness? He will dissipate it. Your attractions? He will chill them. Your cup of delights? He will poison it. Your idolatrous attachments? He will bring separation, sickness and death against them until the day when, deprived of the creature, you will at last throw yourself onto his fatherly bosom, even if it be through weariness, thirst, and despair. His desire is that you might learn to cry out with the psalmist: "Whom have I in heaven but you? And there is nothing on earth that I desire besides you. My flesh and my heart may fail, but God is the rock of my heart and my portion forever" (Psalm 73:25-26 marginal reading). He is my portion *because* he is the rock of my heart; a rock on which this heart can lean all of its weight without fear of ever seeing it give way!

---

³ "There is a void in the heart of man, and God alone can fill it." (Erskine) [A.M.] [Thomas Erskine was the Scotsman who was God's agent in causing Monod's faith to come alive.]

The God Who Loves

"My son, give your heart to me;" to me who began by giving you my heart before asking for yours.

A Selfless Love

Love calls to love, and that is the most irresistible call of all. Someone says to you, "You are required to love that person," and your heart may not yield itself. It might even experience a temptation to resist, through the secret pleasure it finds in affirming its freedom. Or someone says to you, "That person is worthy of your love," and while recognizing the right he has over you, your heart may feel restrained, as if in spite of itself, through a lack of natural attraction. But let someone say to you, "That person loves you with the most tender of loves. He has risked his fortune, his health, his life for you, with no thought of personal benefit or even of repayment," behold, your heart is won over in an instant by the instinctive horror that ingratitude inspires in the human conscience, even an unregenerate one.

This condition of love is never completely fulfilled by the creature, either because he doesn't find in you any more of what such a great heart requires than you find in him, or because there is in him, as there is in you, a core of coldness and of egoism which mixes self-seeking even in its most abandoned devotions. But God has fulfilled that condition, truly fulfilled it. If you ask what he is, Saint John replies, "God is love" (1 John 4:8,16), and if you ask what he has done, the same Saint John answers in the same place, "He first loved us" (1 John 4:19). That is what breaks the heart once it has believed the gospel, the good news of God's love through Jesus Christ. The thing that makes Christians like Saint John—if you will allow me this expression—is the ability to say with Saint John, "We have come to know and to believe the love that God has for us" (1 John 4:16).

Love on the Cross

You would see that love of God everywhere and always, if only you had eyes to see. You would see God's love giving itself, the first to give itself, giving itself without reserve. But do you want to find it fully proclaimed? Then follow the apostle of love on Golgotha, for it is there in front of the cross that he wrote the words I just read to you.

Someone has said, "In creation God shows us his hand; in redemption he gives us his heart." No doubt this antithesis is somewhat forced, and I would argue on the side of creation. No, God's heart is not absent in nature. It throbs in the stirrings of the human soul, in the beating of a mother's heart, in the precious fruit of a rich soil, in the rain from heaven, in the fruitful seasons, and even in the satisfied hunger of the little birds (see Psalm 145).

But it is quite true that the tokens of love that God gave us in creation pale beside those he has given us in redemption, just as the nighttime stars are extinguished for us in the brightness of the day, without, in reality, giving way to it. In going directly to the cross of Jesus Christ to show you "what kind of love the Father has given to us" (see 1 John 3:1) we will only be imitating Saint John and all the apostles. The verb "to give," a favorite word in the gospel, can be replaced by no other, and if Saint John chose it, it is because he saw more in the love of the cross than a sentiment declaring itself. He saw a heart that was giving itself.

My dear listener, have you ever really placed yourself in front of the cross of Jesus Christ? Have you ever pondered the love that God gave you in that mysterious hour when the cry of sacrificial love, "It is finished!" resounded across vast space and eternal ages? It is said that the pious Moravian reformer dated his consecration to God from the day when, crossing a gallery adorned with pictures, he stopped by chance—"I am speaking in human terms" (Romans 6:19)—

before a painting showing the Lord Jesus dying on the cross. These words were written at the bottom: "See what I have done for you; and you, what have you done for me?" The thought of what God gave us on that cross, contemplated seriously for the first time, won the heart of Zinzendorf that day, and with his heart it won his life.

Oh, if only this discourse could be for you what that painting was for Zinzendorf! And why shouldn't it be? Why should you and I not count on the truth of the gospel, on the Spirit of God, and on your heart, if you have one? No elaborate verbal painting of the sufferings of your Savior, no emotional appeal to nervous sensibility. Just the fact, the simple fact of redemption speaking to your emotions and your reason about what this God who asks for your heart has already given you. "God shows his love for us in that while we were still sinners, Christ died for us" (Romans 5:8).

CHRIST DIED FOR US

Christ died for us; I need nothing more.

Christ—that Son of God, his only and beloved son; that other self "with whom he is well pleased" (see Matthew 17:5); that God become man in order to give himself without hindrance to man. Who will tell us his true name? Who will tell us of his divine glory? Who will tell us of his tender relationship with the Father? Who will tell us of these things when even the seraphim cover their faces with their wings in order to hide themselves from the brightness of his majesty (see Isaiah 6:2)? As for us, once we have tried to imagine the most exalted, the most sanctified love of the most loving father for the most loveable son, and to imagine that love silently ascending Mount Moriah,[4] how can we disguise the

---

[4] Mount Moriah is where Abraham went in order to sacrifice Isaac, his only son, his promised son, the son whom he loved (see Genesis 22).

fact that all of that is as much below the mysterious reality as earth is below heaven and man is below God! Oh, inexpressible gift!

Christ *died*—that death, that cruel tearing of the body that scarcely comes to mind next to that bitterness of soul which is a thousand times crueler; that burden of all of the sins of the human race weighing on one single head, the only innocent head; that curse of Sinai[5] swooping down with all its terrors on "the Lamb of God" and made all the more striking by the victim's human holiness and by his divine grandeur. What earthly death could approach it? What earthly sympathy could reply to it? What earthly imagination could conceive of it? When you have tried to assemble in your mind all that you have experienced and known and heard and dreamt concerning human suffering, what will become of that drop of water in the abyss of anguish that resounds with that mournful cry, "My God, my God, why have you forsaken me?" (Matthew 27:46). Oh, inexpressible sacrifice!

Christ died *for us*—for you, for me, for us all. For us who are holy, submissive, and faithful? No, but for us who are sinners, rebels, enemies; for us who only live in order to cause offense and who have, by our crimes, fixed him to that cross where he came to atone for them. For us, at least, who are repentant, believing, praying? No, but for us who are unrepentant, unbelieving, "having no hope and without God in the world" (Ephesians 2:12); for us who have begun to sense our unrighteousness and our peril only upon learning at what price God has redeemed us from the one and withdrawn us from the other. "Is this the manner of man" (2 Samuel 7:19 KJV)? And what are "our ways beside the ways" of that completely free grace, or "our thoughts beside his thoughts" (see Isaiah 55:8). Oh, inexpressible mercy!

---

[5] Mount Sinai was where Moses received the law and the 10 commandments, God's standard for holiness and righteousness that humanity has violated.

The Marvel of an Unresponsive Heart

If only I might return with you to the original source of the love that was revealed to the world through the cross. If only I could go right back before the ages and penetrate into those impenetrable sanctuaries where the councils of the mighty God are held (see Psalm 73:17). If only I could cause you to listen to that deliberation of the Father, the Son, and the Holy Spirit where the redemption of fallen man is determined from time eternal and where love's work is divided between the Father who calls us, the Son who redeems us, and the Spirit who sanctifies us! (1 Peter 1:2)

Angels from heaven, you who are present at the church's gatherings (see Ephesians 3:10), speak. Has nothing come to you from this council of love? No word, no thought, no wayward ray of light that could reveal the gift of God to those hearts whom nothing has yet been able to touch? And if the laws that govern our relationship with you while we are still shut up in these mortal bodies do not permit you to bring news of that divine deliberation from heaven to earth, then come, let me give you news about another deliberation to carry from earth to heaven. It is completely human, but at least as amazing!

Go and tell the celestial beings that, in agreement with you, with Scripture, with the truth of God, and with the conscience of man, I am proclaiming here the love of a God who sent his Son into the world. Tell them that while I do so, there is in front of me a lost sinner debating within himself as to whether or not he should give his heart to the God who gave him his Son. Tell them that in order to make up his mind, this sinner is waiting until he can escape from the influence of a message that is too much in control of him or not enough in control of itself. Tell them that he will be able to tell you tomorrow what side he has come down on. Go and tell them, and you, who so often find earth to be incredulous of word coming from heaven, will find for the first time that heaven is incredulous of word coming from earth!

The God Who Asks

"My son, give your heart to me;" to me who asks it of you.

We Love Because He is Love

Who asks it of you . . . If my goal were simply to defend God's rights over the heart he asks for, I would only need to remind you that he is the one who made it and that, in asking for it, he is merely asking for something that came from him in the first place. I was just saying that the God of Jesus Christ began giving us his heart in creation, but he has done more. He has put that heart in each one of us. Love, which is the most beautiful definition of God, is also the most beautiful gift that God has given to man. If the creature is loving, it is because the Creator is love. And who, then, has the first rights over that power to love if it is not the one who placed it in us along with his own image?

What! That eagerness of devotion, that warmth of affection, that need for communion, all those feelings that are at once so intense and so tender, those feelings through which he has not only revealed himself but also depicted himself within us—all that should be for the rest of the world and not for him? Away with that impious wandering and that excess of ingratitude! But the more it is detestable, the less I feel the need to dwell on it. There is a more delicate concern that I want to present to you here, and I want, in concluding, to appeal to that which is most sensitive and intimate in man's heart.

His Infinite Condescension

When God appears before you and says to you, "My son, give your heart to me;" when he recognizes in you a heart to give and invites you—if I may put it that way—to grant him first place, doesn't it seem to you that the roles are reversed through an infinite condescension? Doesn't it seem to you that you are hearing today something like a prayer from God that man can grant; that you are called, for the very first time, to do something for him who has done everything for you?

Far, far be it from us—do I need to say it?— to have any thought that could in the least diminish the infinite grandeur, the unchangeable bliss of the King of kings. He doesn't need man to serve him or the son of man to come to his aid. "Is it any pleasure to the Almighty if you are in the right, or is it gain to him if you make your ways blameless?" (Job 22:3). But God's grandeur is not, after all, an insensitive grandeur, nor is God's bliss a cold and impassive bliss. The God of Jesus Christ is a living God in whom there moves a spirit of love and sympathy. Well, how can we represent that love, that sympathy to ourselves, other than by transferring to God feelings analogous to those in man; transferring them while disengaging them from all that is tainted by sin and the flesh so as to retain only that which is, in its essence, living and personal?

Nevertheless, in contemplating this marvel of love—a Creator and Savior God who asks for the heart of his sinful and lost creature—let us, like Moses before the burning bush, be fearful of coming too close. Without pretending to raise a presumptuous eye to the divine nature, let us rest our gaze on this God who has made man expressly for the purpose of placing himself at our disposal, and let us contemplate the Father's heart through the human heart of the Son who said to us, "Whoever has seen me has seen the Father" (John 14:9). Can you imagine Jesus being unmoved at the sight of a repentant sinner who comes to give him his heart? Unmoved? The one who compares himself to the good shepherd going "after the [sheep] that is lost, until he finds it?

And when he has found it, he lays it on his shoulders, rejoicing. And when he comes home, he calls together his friends and his neighbors, saying to them, 'Rejoice with me, for I have found my sheep that was lost' " (Luke 15:4-6)! Don't you want to give him that joy?

The Joy We Can Give

When Jesus, "wearied . . . from his journey" and sitting beside Jacob's well, says to the Samaritan woman, "Give me a drink" (John 4:6-7), who among you does not envy that woman the privilege of being able to give her Savior a cup of cold water to quench his thirst? But you will have no reason to envy her if, through the gift of your heart, you respond to that deeper, more spiritual "I thirst" (John 19:28) that escapes from him on the cross where he died for you.

When Jesus says to Zacchaeus, "Hurry and come down, for I must stay at your house today" (Luke 19:5), who among you does not envy Zacchaeus the privilege of receiving his Savior into his home and lavishing all of his cares on him? But you will have no reason to envy him if you open your heart to this same Savior who says to you today, "I stand at the door and knock. If anyone hears my voice and opens the door, I will come in and eat with him, and he with me" (Revelation 3:20).

When Jesus succumbs beneath the heavy instrument of his punishment, who among you does not envy Simon of Cyrene the privilege of carrying for a few minutes that cross on which his Savior will soon bear our sins in his body (1 Peter 2:24)? But you will have no reason to envy him if you are among those in whom he gathers the fruit of "the anguish of his soul" (Isaiah 53:11) and if your heart is part of the precious "spoil" that is his "portion with . . . the strong, because he poured out his soul to death" (Isaiah 53:12, marginal reading).

And when this same Jesus, already crucified and having just been resurrected from the dead, says to Peter, "Simon, son of John, do you love me?" (John 21:17), which of you does not envy the fallen apostle, who has been raised up again, the privilege of pouring the "oil and wine" (Luke 10:34) of his repentance and love into the wounds that he helped inflict in the body and soul of his Savior? But you will have no reason to envy the apostle if, eager to bring a measure of joy to the one for whom you have caused so much pain, your heart flies, like Peter's, to meet the question posed by his Master and yours, so that you, in turn, say to him, "Lord, you know everything; you know that I love you" (John 21:17).

Those Who Hesitate

Is there someone here who feels otherwise about this? Is there someone who, in the Samaritan woman's place, would have refused the cup of cold water; someone who, in Zacchaeus' place, would have kept his door closed; someone who, in Simon of Cyrene's place, would have left the cross on the shoulders that bore it; someone who, in Peter's place, would have responded, well, differently from Peter? If so, he will only be consistent with himself in resisting the invitation of my text and continuing to deny the God of Jesus Christ the heart for which he is asking.

Why Would You Refuse?

Deny him? And why? When you have denied him the heart for which he is asking, what will you do with it? Speak. Explain yourself. Do you dare to stand up in this congregation and tell us what more worthy object would cause you to rob God of the heart that he requests? "Be appalled, O heavens, at this; be shocked, be utterly desolate," declares the Lord, "for my people have committed two evils: they have forsaken me, the fountain of living waters, and hewed out cisterns for themselves, broken cisterns that can hold no water" (Jeremiah 2:12-13). That is precisely your unworthy history! That is the bitter outrage you have committed against the living and true God!

A few days ago a devout missionary told us the touching story of the Bassoutus who were suddenly brought "from darkness to light" (Acts 26:18), "from death to life" (John 5:24), "and from the power of Satan to God" (Acts 26:18). Let one of them lend me his voice. "God told the sun to shine, and it shone; he told the grass to sprout, and it sprouted; he told the rivers to flow and they flowed; he said to man, 'love me,' and man refused to obey!"

But what have I been doing for the last hour? I have been gathering the strongest reasons, choosing the most touching expressions, urging, entreating. Who have I been entreating and for what? Has it been for God to pardon sinful man and give him his heart, which is all too justly alienated from us? No, I have been entreating sinful man to give his heart to the God of Jesus Christ; to the God for whom that heart hungers and thirsts; to the God who has fully given us his own heart; to the God who seems to have need of ours in order to complete his bliss of love. What? Isn't that taking unnecessary care?

Alas, let us rather fear that it is taking useless care.

Give God Your Heart

Oh, my brother, my sister, give the world today the only moral spectacle more lovely than that of an angel who has never stopped loving God. Give it the spectacle of a sinner, an enemy who has become a friend. Give it the spectacle of a Saint Peter, just recently apostate, to whom Jesus says, "Do you love me?" and who answers him, "You know that I love you." Give it the spectacle of a Mary Magdalene, just recently possessed with seven demons, to whom Jesus says, "Mary," and who answers him "Rabboni." Give that spectacle to the world today while waiting to give it to the universe on the day of judgment. Yes, be that Saint Peter, be that Mary. You can, if you want to. Man refuses God's heart every day, but God has never refused man's heart. He doesn't solicit it, awaken it, and touch it in order to refuse it. Only desire, and you will give him your heart. Desire and you have already given it.

As for you, elder brothers who have already returned, go and embrace that prodigal child retracing the path to the father's home. "Greet [him] with the kiss of love" (1 Peter 5:14). Encourage his still wavering steps. Above all, above all, spare him the scandal of your dead profession and know for certain whether you yourselves have truly given your hearts to God!

And you, eternal Father, who sees him "while he [is] still a long way off" (Luke 15:20), come out to meet him, and while he is pouring out on your bosom his humble confession, "Father, I have sinned against heaven and before you. I am no longer worthy to be called your son" (Luke 15:21), may he sense the beat of your father-heart against his son-heart, and may he hear this fatherly cry coming from your mouth, "This my son was dead, and is alive again; he was lost, and is found!" (Luke 15:24). Amen.

ARE YOU THIRSTY?

ల

(Paris, 1849)

John 7:37

On the last day of the Feast, the great day, Jesus stood up and cried out, "If anyone thirsts, let him come to me and drink."

A HEAVENLY INVITATION

Is there someone here who is thirsty? Is there someone who thirsts for enjoyment and has never been able to find the pleasures that can satisfy him? Is there someone who thirsts for enlightenment and has never been able to understand anything to its depths? Is there someone who thirsts for love and has never been able to exchange all of his heart for the whole heart of another? Is there someone who thirsts for holiness and has never been able fully to disengage himself from the entanglements of sin? Finally, is there someone who has been consumed up to now in the pursuit of a goal he has been unable to attain and that he despairs of ever attaining?

"Come, everyone who thirsts" (Isaiah 55:1), lend an ear to Jesus Christ, your brother and your God; your brother in order to feel your pain, and your God in order to heal it. He is calling you in the name of that thirst which devours you, so that he might satisfy you in himself and so that the emptier you are when you come to him, the fuller you will be when he sends you away: "If anyone thirsts, let him come to me and drink" (John 7:37).

There are words spoken by the Holy Spirit that one fears to spoil by touching them, and it is only with a sort of reluctance that I take the risk of unfolding this tender invitation from the Savior. I would rather limit myself to that instinctive eagerness with which each of you has just opened himself up to this invitation, like parched ground to a soaking rain. I hesitate to add human reasoning that can only be grasped when something of earth's heaviness is mixed with the heavenly anointing.

Thus, I would willingly make myself a "Quaker" before my text. I would prefer a half hour of silence to all the discourses, provided I could flatter myself that the half hour would be spent in those "groanings too deep for words" through which "the Spirit himself intercedes for us" (Romans 8:26). But I have such confidence for only a few of you. Therefore, that which the majority would not do on their own, I have it on my heart to do, not for them but with them. I do so with more than the usual desire to bring you not the product of human wisdom but the fruit of God's Word examined through prayer and commented on through experience.

Our Unquenched Thirst

Thirst supposes two things: a felt need on the inside and nothing to satisfy it on the outside. If this need found something to satisfy it on the outside, thirst would give way to fulfillment and would become a source of well-being. If the need were not felt on the inside, thirst would give way to indifference and would at least cease to be a source of grief. But to wish without obtaining, to seek without finding, to desire without being able—that is thirst. Alas, that is also the present condition of mankind; that is our condition, yours and mine. In our hearts there is an enormous void, and in life nothing to fill it. At the very most we find a few paltry and deceptive contentments that throw themselves into this void only to be lost there, the way a dry leaf is lost in the Niagara River.

Our hearts! What is more insatiable, but also what is less satisfied? Try to name just one of our aspirations that isn't turned into bitterness by the deceptions that it encounters. All those thirsts that torment us and that the reading of my text sufficed to awaken in you are just so many natural faculties that cried out to life but life didn't answer.

The Thirst for Enjoyment

The thirst for enjoyment is the desperation of our unsatisfied ability to feel. Let us leave to "what is falsely called 'knowledge' " (1 Timothy 6:20) its superb and superficial disdain for the physical man. In the plans of a Creator who "is good to all" (Psalm 145:9), the parts of this body—the dwelling place and instrument of man's spirit—should be nothing but the means of legitimate enjoyment and of happy as well as helpful activity.

What have they become in reality? I hope they have not been subjected to pain through sickness or accident. At the very least, however, they have become blunted, used up, destroyed by age—that is, by the normal and appropriate maturing of our being. What a strange and cruel thing! The very progression of life is responsible for casting us outside of the pleasant things for which life was loaned to us, until, at last, it casts us outside of life itself.

I thirst.

The Thirst for Enlightenment

The thirst for enlightenment is the desperation of our unsatisfied ability to understand. This curious need to inquire into the world, into ourselves, and into the invisible God who made all things is something that we bring into the world at birth. This need is equally felt in innocent childhood, where it gives instruction a natural point of departure, and in studious maturity, where it serves as a goad for all research and a foundation for all learning. This need won't stop until it comes to the farthest reaches of time and space and unravels all the great problems of the human spirit. Even then it can't stop. It can only live by marching on and would rather throw itself recklessly into the void than deny itself by saying, "That is enough."

Why is there this immense apparatus? It is to arrive, in the end, at the little that you or I know—poor creatures that we are, bounded in front by weakness and behind by weariness; to the right by the shortness of time and to the left by the necessities of life; hemmed in on all sides by an invincible ignorance.

I thirst.

The Thirst for Love

The thirst for love is the desperation of our unsatisfied ability to love. If there is anything that distinguishes us from creatures of a lower order, anything that allows us to be recognized as the offspring of God, "in whom we live and move and have our being" (see Acts 17:28), anything that makes us savor the feeling, the bliss, the glory of our existence, without doubt that thing is love. Love is that mysterious and tender faculty we possess of doubling life by getting out of ourselves in order to live in another. When we love not with that self-interested or covetous love which is just egoism in disguise, but rather with that love whose principle and model lie in God, then to love is to reflect the image of a "God [who] is love" (1 John 4:8,16); to love is to make heaven descend to earth.

Yes, but this heaven on earth, where is it? Love such as man's heart cries out for and longs for—a love that charms it without seducing it, floods it without intoxicating it, possesses it without robbing it of itself; a love that is true, pure, holy, divine—where do we find it, where do we even seek it down here? Tell me, if you know!

I thirst.

THE THIRST FOR HOLINESS

The thirst for holiness is the desperation of our unsatisfied ability to do what is right. If the spirit is the spice of life and the heart is its charm, then the conscience is its prize. The supreme ambition to imitate the thrice holy God, the determined resolve to submit everything to his will and to regulate everything according to his law, come what may, that is the deepest, most imperious, most inalienable need of human nature. No doubt, you also take it to be the most assured of being completely satisfied because of God's faithfulness.

Completely satisfied! Alas, do you not see the bitter smile that this hope evokes from the very best in the world, who also happen to be the most discontented with themselves? Then believe a man who has most likely never been surpassed in holiness and has perhaps never been equaled. Listen to Saint Paul, as he groans so painfully through the Holy Spirit.

> The law is spiritual, but I am of the flesh, sold under sin. I do not understand my own actions. For I do not do what I want, but I do the very thing I hate. . . . For I know that nothing good dwells in me, that is, in my flesh. For I have the desire to do what is right, but not the ability to

carry it out. For I do not do the good I want, but the evil I do not want is what I keep on doing. ... So I find it to be a law, that when I want to do right, evil lies close at hand. For I delight in the law of God, in my inner being, but I see in my members another law waging war against the law of my mind and making me captive to the law of sin that dwells in my members. — Romans 7:14-15,18-19,21-23

When someone like Saint Paul speaks, or rather weeps, that way over the state of human nature, it would be superfluous to gather together, one by one, the humiliating confessions of the likes of Socrates or Kant, of Augustine or Luther. Besides, you don't need any other testimony than that of your own conscience examined in good faith. When have you attained, when have you even come close to attaining the ideal of holiness that you carry within you? When have you been able to restrain your thoughts, your speech, even your actions under the one divine law? When have you been able to do all that you desired, all that you should—I almost said, all that you could? Ah, who would not recognize, if only he were honest with himself, that this point where the satisfaction of our inner desires is most necessary—and apparently most promised—is also the point where it most invariably escapes us? Who can recall what he is supposed to be with regard to godliness, charity, purity, and patience without crying out to himself in the most intimate depths of his soul:

"I thirst"?

Two Options

I thirst. It is there that we must always end, each time that we compare the needs of the heart with the realities of life. The disproportion—I was going to say, the contrast—is so great between the two halves of our existence that one can scarcely persuade himself that they were made for one another. One would be tempted to believe, to the extent that he hasn't learned the secret of this schism from the gospel, that his heart was made for another world or this world was made for another heart and that they have only been thrown together through a bizarre, blind mix-up.

This perpetual contradiction between heart and life is intolerable in the long run. To remain there is impossible; we must get out at all cost. Yet, in order to get out, man has only two options: either discover a life that has risen to the level of the heart or, if such a life doesn't exist, lower the heart to the level of life.

Lower Our Heart's Desires?

Lower the heart to the level of life; that is the ordinary recourse of nine tenths of the human race. The heart is too large for life? Never mind! We will put the heart in its place; we will cut it down until it knows how to adjust its demands to the gifts of life, just as one prunes the over-luxuriant boughs of a tree until it fits nicely into the arbors of Versailles.

Our physical being has an ability to feel that is capable of sweet and delicate delights but that finds no contentment worthy of it in the things of earth. Very well, we must be content with less and reduce the admirable machinery of our natural man to animal dimensions, restricted to the satisfaction of our needs and appetites.

Our spirit has an ability to question and understand that never wearies of searching and that discovers no place of rest for itself here on earth. Very well, we must wean this importunate curiosity, turning aside the thirst for study into a passion for business speculations or political discussions. We must train our misguided intelligence to turn endlessly and fruitlessly in on itself, like the unfortunate squirrel condemned to dizzy himself without respite in the stationary movement of the wheel that serves as his cage.

Our heart has an ability to love that the best creatures can only aggravate by their impotence to satisfy it. Very well, we must say farewell to love; we must make for ourselves a less difficult heart. In the matter of our affections, we must learn to make do with the measure we have received.

Our conscience has an ability for holy obedience that knows of nothing too high for its sublime flight, but that cannot try to take wing without colliding at every turn with either the hidden stumbling blocks in the depths of the soul, or the suggestions of the evil one, or the maxims of a corrupt society. Very well, we must clip its wings; we must teach it to get along without an unrealistic perfection. We must resign ourselves to live as everyone else lives and to make peace with ourselves, provided that we avoid going astray into gross sensuality, sordid greed, foolish extravagance, or wanton egoism.

One doesn't say all that to himself, but he acts in that spirit. One doesn't propose this ignoble goal to himself, but a vague instinct leads him in that direction, and, alas, he ends up reaching it.

Raise Our Lives!

But let us not be too hard on human nature. It is more worthy of pity than of indignation here. Once again, the force of circumstances drags us along and even compels us to put heart and life into agreement. Our only recourse is to gradually extinguish our heart in the suffocating atmosphere of life, unless, on the contrary, we know of a way to renew life through the hearth of the heart. Instead of lowering the heart to the level of life, raise life to the level of the heart. There, there is the only solution to this terrible problem that is worthy of us, because it is the only one able to satisfy us without humiliating us.

But is this solution possible? It is, because it must be. It is, because something within us tells us on God's behalf that it is. It is, because God, through the agency of his Son, that other self, declares to us that it is. "If anyone thirsts . . ." what should he do? Stifle his thirst? No, but give it free reign and satisfy it in Jesus Christ. "If anyone thirsts, let him come to me and drink." Thus there is, thanks be to God, a life that fully answers all the needs of the human heart, with its most exalted instincts. That life is in Jesus Christ and is communicated to us through faith.

Our Thirst Quenched in Jesus Christ

Who among all the men whom our earth has nourished has offered in his person the most complete example—or, rather, the most complete pattern—of inner peace and harmony? You have answered, "the man Christ Jesus" (1 Timothy 2:5), which is the name that Saint Paul gives to the Son of God considered in the humble perfection of his human nature. This peace and harmony imply that the heart of the man Jesus Christ, unlike our own, had found a life that satisfied it on every point. What was that life?

Not His Earthly Life

It wasn't his earthly life. Looking only at his earthly life, the man Jesus Christ is, of all men, the one in whom the disparity I just discussed between our inner needs and outer contentment was surely the most complete and, at the same time, the most keenly sensed. None other had a heart so large, yet for none other was life so bitter. Pilate depicted Jesus Christ more faithfully than he knew in saying to the Jews, "Behold the man!" (John 19:5). Jesus Christ is not only a man, he is *the* man; the most man of men; the man in whom the whole of humanity is summed up and who carries its distinctive qualities to their highest level. All the parts of his being—conscience, heart, spirit, even his body—must have been provided with an exquisite capacity and delicacy that, while opening him more than another to the sweetness—dare I say the enjoyments?—for which normal humanity is formed, also made him more subject than another to feeling the bitterness and privations reserved for fallen humanity.

Thus, when this Son of man neared the ultimate time when all was to be accomplished for him and through him, he released the sigh, "I thirst" (John 19:28), which the divine Scriptures had announced a thousand years earlier (Psalm 69:21). His words expressed—does it need to be said?—more than a material need that a little water drawn from the bosom of our poor earth would satisfy. Jesus' physical thirst is the emblem of another, greater, and more hidden thirst that troubles his entire human nature. Thirst for bliss, thirst for light, thirst for love, thirst for holiness—all the thirsts that consume us focus their passion in him. No one will ever experience anything like his need to enjoy existence in all its purity or to gaze upon truth in all its brilliance or to love and be loved without reservation or to taste God's fellowship without a shadow.

Is this thirst of thirsts assuaged? Alas, a sponge soaked in vinegar is all that the divine crucified one is given in his agony by the mercy of his executioners! This, too, was foreseen in the same verse in Scripture: "They gave me poison for food, and for my thirst they gave me sour wine to drink" (Psalm 69:21). But this gall and vinegar are, in turn, emblems of the answer that earth gives to the thirst that consumes the Son of man.

To his thirst for bliss, earth responds with a cup that he cannot see approaching his lips without recoiling from it and crying out, "My Father, if it be possible, let this cup pass from me" (Matthew 26:39).

To his thirst for light, it responds with a darkness that veils the face of the sun—a mysterious token of that other darkness that, in this gloomy hour, conceals the plans of divine justice. In the midst of this darkness, the Son of God himself can scarcely find his way: "Hide not your face from your servant" (Psalm 69:17); "My heart throbs; . . . and the light of my eyes—it also has gone from me" (Psalm 38:10).

To his thirst for love, calling out through his atoning sacrifice to a cursed and fallen earth, that ungrateful earth responds with an indifference that turns away from the victim, with a cowardice that abandons him, a treason that betrays him, a hatred that condemns him, and a rage that slaughters him. "They have pierced my hands and feet" (Psalm 22:16). "My close friend . . . has lifted his heel against me" (Psalm 41:9). "I looked for pity, but there was none, and for comforters, but I found none" (Psalm 69:20).

And finally, suppose he seeks refuge in the bosom of his God and Father. To his thirst for holy communion with his God and Father, earth responds with sins, sins without number or measure which it piles onto his innocent head. These sins call down upon him the full heavenly retribution. They press with an insupportable weight on the very prayer of his soul: "My iniquities have gone over my head; like a heavy burden, they are too heavy for me" (Psalm 38:4), "My God, my God, why have you forsaken me? Why are you so far from saving me, from the words of my groaning?" (Psalm 22:1).

HIS ETERNAL, HEAVENLY LIFE!

But if the earthly life of the man Jesus Christ irritates his thirst rather than satisfying it, once again, what is that other life that quenches his thirst, that waters it, that floods it with peace and harmony? It is the life he contemplates in Psalm 16, the life following his resurrection from the dead: "You make known to me the path of life" (Psalm 16:11). It is the life that the Father promised him in Isaiah as the reward for the sacrifice of his earthly life: "When his soul makes an offering for sin, . . . he shall prolong his days" (Isaiah 53:10). Finally it is the life through which the apostle explains to us the secret of his renunciation of this world's life and glory: "Looking to Jesus, the founder and perfecter of our faith, who for the joy that was set before him endured the cross, despising the shame, and is seated at the right hand of the throne of God" (Hebrews 12:2).

Looking past his earthly life made transparent by faith, Jesus discovers a further life which he will enter on the coming day. It is a life that was made for his heart, just as his heart was made for it; a life for which his thirst need only wait in order to be fully satisfied. If he thirsts for bliss, behold, in this new life, there is "fullness of joy in God's presence; at his right hand are pleasures forevermore" (see Psalm 16:11). If he thirsts for light, behold all the veils are lifted, and the fullness of divine truth shines radiantly in him and for him. If he thirsts for love, behold the family of his redeemed return to him love for love, retelling among themselves and with the holy angels the lesson of love they have learned from him. If he thirsts for communion with God, behold the Father filling up the Son with his unspeakable affection, and the Father's holy will being accomplished through the Son in the liberated and renewed creation (see Romans 8:21).

"Come Unto Me"

This is the one who says to you who are thirsting today as he thirsted, "If anyone thirsts, let him come to me and drink" (John 7:37). It is not for himself alone that he has won this eternal life where the harmony of his existence, broken by his earthly life, is reestablished. He won it for his poor fallen creatures, who have ruined their lives and troubled the earth through their sin.

Let them only believe in him. Let them throw themselves without reserve into the arms of this Son of God who has become the Son of man in order to redeem them. Let them desire "to know nothing . . . except Jesus Christ and him crucified" (1 Corinthians 2:2)—no other righteousness than his obedience, no other expiation than his sacrifice, no other salvation than his grace, his totally free grace (see Romans 3:24). That is all that is necessary for him to share with them all that he has received from the Father and for him to impart to them the divine life that he has earned for them in place of the death that they have drawn upon him.

In the most prophetic of all the prophetic psalms, he has scarcely begun to rejoice in the deliverance that God reserves for him after all his suffering, when he suddenly turns from himself to his "brothers," guaranteeing them that their hearts will live in his. "May your hearts live forever" (Psalm 22:26). He takes up this promise again in Saint John after the lapse of eleven centuries: "Because I live, you also will live" (John 14:19). "Whoever has the Son has life" (1 John 5:12). He has the life of the Son, the life that corresponds to our heart, the life that at last is life. If today this "life is hidden with Christ in God" (Colossians 3:3), we need only wait for tomorrow in order to see it come to light. "When Christ who is your life appears, then you also will appear with him in glory" (Colossians 3:4). There, in Jesus' life that has become yours, and there alone will you find something to quench the thirst that consumes you.

Our Thirst Satisfied

You thirst for holiness, and here is something to satisfy you. What could disturb your obedience? The sight before your eyes? You have inherited "new heavens and a new earth in which righteousness dwells" (2 Peter 3:13) under the rule of Jesus. The tempter? Where you are going he cannot follow (see John 13:36), and he no longer has anything in you because he has nothing in Jesus (see John 14:30). Your own corruption? It has given way to God's Spirit filling you with that measureless measure which is Jesus' portion (see John 3:34). The people around you? You are in the company of earth's elect, now freed from sin, and of the heavenly angels who never knew it. Beyond that, you are in the company of Jesus who is worshiped by both and of whom it is said, "We shall be like him, because we shall see him as he is" (1 John 3:2). Pure as he is pure, holy as he is holy, one with him as he is one with the Father, you no longer "hunger and thirst for righteousness" except to "be satisfied" (Matthew 5:6) and to be "filled with all the fullness of God" (Ephesians 3:19).

You thirst for love, and here is something to satisfy you. You have been unable to find a creature down here who is loveable and loving enough to answer the capacity of your heart, but in front of this "Son of man who is in heaven" (John 3:13, marginal reading) the problem is just the reverse. He is loveable enough to be the "delight" (Proverbs 8:30) of eternal love, and he is loving "to the point of death, even death on a cross" (Philippians 2:8). You seek in vain within yourself for a heart able to contain all the love that he inspires in you and that overflows from you on all sides. This does not even mention the love that the creatures themselves henceforth inspire in you, after and in your love for him, by virtue of having been sanctified and transformed into his likeness. In the bosom of that heavenly family, of which no family on earth can give us any idea, you will live in love, you will live love, and you will be love as God himself is.

You thirst for light, and here is something to satisfy you. What would be lacking in your need to know if, each day, you could converse with and question Jesus, "in whom are hidden all the treasures of wisdom and knowledge" (Colossians 2:3)? Your need would be met as soon as it was felt. Very well, here you are, admitted to his everyday conversations; here you are, free to question him as much as you like. But Jesus promises you still more. "In that day you will ask nothing of me" (John 16:23), because nothing will be able to elude your searches or, to put it better, hide itself from your sight, filled as it is with the living light of God.

Finally, you thirst for real happiness, a happiness that fulfills the whole man, and here again is something to satisfy you. The bliss that Jesus reserves for you in the place he has gone to prepare for you (John 14:2) is for the whole man— for his resurrected body as well as for his sanctified spirit. Philosophy—if it promised anything at all!—has nothing to offer you but a cold immortality in which the soul, separated from the body, can at most claim an incomplete and incomprehensible existence which it seemingly must consume in running after the other half of itself, which is no longer there. The gospel of Jesus, on the other hand, calls you to live again complete in a body that the apostle calls successively "heavenly," "glorious," "imperishable," and, finally, "spiritual" (see 1 Corinthians 15:40-44), as if he despaired of defining it except through an indefinable contradiction. You will live in a body all of whose abilities, at once both exalted and purified, are equally suited to serve for God's glory and for your own well being. Finally, you will live in a body that you nourish with "fresh fruit" (Ezekiel 47:12) seated "at table with Abraham, Isaac, and Jacob in the kingdom of heaven" (Matthew 8:11), beholding, face to face, the object of their faith and yours (see Job 19:25-27).

What more can I say? As you lean over this inexhaustible well of holiness, love, light, and joy in Jesus, you need only bend down to drink long draughts of all that you thirst for, all that you could ever thirst for.

His Promises are Sure

But what am I doing trying to depict things that "no eye has seen, nor ear heard, nor the heart of man imagined" (1 Corinthians 2:9)? Rather, let us hold fast to the word of our Savior. "He knows our frame" (Psalm 103:14) as well as the thirst he has come to share with us, and he promises that we will be satisfied. That should be enough for us.

What's more, his promise is nothing new. He promised it yesterday, in the magnificent language of the early prophets announcing his first coming:

> When the poor and needy seek water,
>   and there is none,
>   and their tongue is parched with thirst,
> I the LORD will answer them;
>   I the God of Israel will not forsake them.
> I will open rivers on the bare heights,
>   and fountains in the midst of the valleys.
> I will make the wilderness a pool of water,
>   and the dry land springs of water."
>
> — Isaiah 41:17-18

He will promise it tomorrow in the tender invitations of the apostle-prophet, announcing his second coming: "To the thirsty I will give from the spring of the water of life without payment" (Revelation 21:6). "The Spirit and the bride say, 'Come.' And let the one who hears say, 'Come.' And let the one who is thirsty come; let the one who desires take the water of life without price" (Revelation 22:17). "They shall hunger no more, neither thirst anymore. . . . For the Lamb in the midst of the throne will be their shepherd, and he will guide them to springs of living water" (Revelation 7:16-17). What more do we need?

Let us endeavor, through the imperfect means at our disposal today, to imagine all that could fill up the empty places of our hearts. But having done so, let us wisely affirm that God "is able to do far more abundantly than all we ask or think" (Ephesians 3:20). Earth is no further below heaven than our most fervent wishes and our boldest hopes are below the living reality that Jesus will cause us to find near him and in him tomorrow, when the veil of this flesh that separates us from him has fallen.

Oh, my soul, yield yourself without fear to the ambition that troubles you! Spread your wings in infinite space! "Open your mouth wide" (Psalm 81:10)! Wish, ask, call out, and don't despair any longer. Don't despair of anything except of the ability to embrace the full enormity of the fulfillment promised for that other life that God placed before his Christ and that his Christ has placed before you: "If anyone thirsts, let him come to me and drink."

Today: A Time of Preparation

Yes, tomorrow; but what about today? Why do we find the barrier of this earthly life so cruelly intercepting the awaited satisfaction, standing between our hearts and the heavenly life that will satisfy them? This earthly life is so short in view of eternity but so long in time, especially when one is suffering. Yet even the sufferings with which it abounds are less of a hindrance to accepting it than is the void and imperfection that it offers to a being who can only rest in fullness and perfection. Why is there the barrier of this earthly life?

To that question I could respond with the disturbance that sin has brought into the work of the Creator and that needs to be recognized in order to be repaired. But here let us cling instead to a happier response, and one more in keeping with the spirit of my text. Today has its designated place in tomorrow's fulfillment. Earthly life only intercepts heavenly life in order to prepare for it. It is not the barrier to heavenly life; it is its apprenticeship and training.

Gaining the Prize

It is once again to the man Christ Jesus that we must go to study this instructive and consoling doctrine. How poorly someone has understood the gospel if, in the earthly life of Jesus Christ, he can only find an obstacle or a delay to the unfolding of his heavenly life! The gospel causes us to contemplate the one as the prelude—I was going to say, the condition—of the other. "We see . . . Jesus, crowned with glory and honor because of the suffering of death" (Hebrews 2:9). It is because "he humbled himself . . . to the point of death, even death on a cross" (Philippians 2:8) that he was sovereignly raised up and that he received "the name that is above every name" (Philippians 2:9). It is the fruit of the "the anguish of his soul" on earth with which he will "be satisfied" (Isaiah 53:11) for ever and ever.

He knows this well, and this thought sweetens the bitterness of his earthly life. Let us go further; this thought inspires in him a holy impatience to go through, to empty the series of pains through which he must pass in order to "enter into his glory" (Luke 24:26). Those pains put off the joy of his deliverance only to ripen and increase it.

There is a cup that he instinctively pushes away, yet, at the same time, he thirsts for it in order to accomplish his mission, and if he cries out, "Father, save me from this hour," he immediately adds, in a contrary sentiment, "But for this purpose I have come to this hour. Father, glorify your name!" (John 12:27-28). There is a baptism of suffering with which he must be baptized, yet he thirsts for it: "I have a baptism to be baptized with, and how great is my distress until it is accomplished!" (Luke 12:50). There is a last Passover that must prefigure his sacrifice and precede it by a few hours, yet he thirsts for it: "I have earnestly desired to eat this Passover with you before I suffer" (Luke 22:15).

He thirsts for the prompt unfolding of the plot that will deliver him into the hands of the wicked: "What you are going to do," he says to Judas, the traitor, "do quickly" (John 13:27). Finally, he thirsts for the whole will of God, which leads to the sacrifice of the cross (see Hebrews 10:9-10): "My food is to do the will of him who sent me and to accomplish his work" (John 4:34). This is a thirst declared long ago in the prophesy, "Behold, I have come; in the scroll of the book it is written of me: I desire to do your will, O my God; your law is within my heart" (Psalm 40:7-8, see Hebrews 10:5-10). Thus, until such time as he can satisfy his thirst in the joy to come, Jesus satisfies it in the present bitterness of which this joy is the prize.

Growing the Fruit

Yet this view is still too superficial. Let us probe deeper into the philosophy of the divine plan, all of whose parts are so marvelously joined together. The heavenly joy of the man Jesus Christ is not only the prize of his earthly bitterness; it is the fruit. The one is not only attached to the other as salary is to work; it is attached as the growth is to the seed. Between the present and the future, Scripture recognizes a natural and necessary relationship that lies at the very heart of things: "Whatever one sows, that he will also reap" (Galatians 6:7). Taken in their deepest essence, the heavenly life of "the man Christ Jesus" (1 Timothy 2:5) and his earthly life are joined and mingled together, for his heavenly life is only the free expansion of the Spirit of God who already fills him without measure in his earthly life (John 3:34), but as though bound up in the flesh.

This Spirit, who alone quenches the thirst of the inner man, is depicted in Scripture symbolically as the water that refreshes the physical man (see Isaiah 44:3; 55:1). This is especially true in our gospel, which explains itself in clear terms following my text: "Now this he said about the Spirit, whom those who believed in him were to receive" (John 7:39). Filled with this Spirit, Jesus first carries out in his own human nature all that he comes to accomplish in humanity. He is so united with his Father, so established in the Kingdom of heaven, that he transports heaven to earth and lives in eternity in the midst of time.

That is how he finds the means, even while still down here, to satisfy the needs of his heart in all the events of his earthly life—events which he sees as all being arranged by God, one after the other. And because there are none more suited to developing God's life in him than those that rend the flesh, as if to open a wider doorway for God's Spirit, so he finds none that can better quench the thirst that assails him. The Spirit, who will satisfy that thirst tomorrow in the peaceful glory of on high, will satisfy it today, even in the terrible but victorious battle he wages against the flesh.

The Unity of Our Earthly and Heavenly Lives

As the master, so the disciples. For us too, the aggravated thirst of today is the necessary preparation, the paternal training that inevitably leads to the satisfied thirst of tomorrow.

For us too, though it was needful that "for a little while" we should be "grieved by various trials, so that the tested genuineness of [our] faith . . . may be found to result in praise and glory and honor at the revelation of Jesus Christ," those trials are mixed with a "joy that is inexpressible and filled with glory" (1 Peter 1:6-8).

For us too, the heavenly life begins down here under the name of spiritual life, through the Spirit with whom Jesus floods our hearts like a river of living water flooding parched ground. The spiritual life is already the heavenly life, but the heavenly life veiled by the visible world. The heavenly life is still the spiritual life, but the spiritual life liberated from the visible world. Thus the gospel uses one and the same name, "eternal life," for both. This life begins on earth in order to be pursued in heaven. Through it, "everyone who lives and believes in [Jesus Christ] shall never die" (John 11:26).[1]

For us too, then, nothing is lost, nothing is postponed by the trials of life. The precious seed, whose fruit will one day be harvested with a triumphant song, is sown in tears (Psalm 126:5). The cross is the only path to glory, and the heaviest crosses are the shortest paths. Once pierced with this doctrine of the gospel—or, more accurately, once animated by the Spirit of Jesus Christ—the Christian soul will taste a kind of joy in the disappointments, the privations, and the sufferings of life because it will sense a deep inner thirst which those disappointments, those privations, those sufferings satisfy in their way. It will learn to say with the indomitable Paul, "For the sake of Christ, then, I am content with weaknesses, insults, hardships, persecutions, and calamities" (2 Corinthians 12:10),[2] and with the tender Hezekiah, "Lord, by these things men live; and in all these is the life of my spirit" (Isaiah 38:16).

Oh, what light, what glory, what bliss flow out of these spiritual heights onto earthly life! To say that "for those who love God all things work together for good" (Romans 8:28) is, no doubt, to say much, but it doesn't say all that is revealed to us here. It is not only that life's troubles are

---

[1] The theme of this paragraph and the message of this last Scripture quotation are developed in greater depth in Chapter 4, "I Am the Resurrection and the Life."

[2] The version of the Bible from which Monod was quoting, like the King James Version in English, makes this an even stronger statement. It has "I take pleasure in . . . " The point is not that we enjoy these difficult and painful things in their own right but that the richness of the fruit they produce outweighs the pain.

turned into healthy trials; the very character of our entire life is transformed and—if you will allow me to say so—is transfigured. Henceforth earthly life, rather than appearing as something indifferent that is scarcely accepted while awaiting something better, appears instead as something which is as perfect in its way as heavenly life is in its own. One could not imagine anything better suited than earthly life to prepare and educate us for heavenly life, and in stripping it of that which aggravates our thirst today, we would strip it of that which most surely guarantees our coming satisfaction.

Earthly life is related to heavenly life almost the way the Old Testament is to the New. The Old Testament appears foreign, incoherent, at times hard until the New Testament has come "not . . . to abolish . . . but to fulfill" (Matthew 5:17). Thus heavenly life, in explaining and continuing earthly life, imbues it with order and harmony and peace.

Those in the Valley of Tears

Out of this consolation that is offered to all, I urge those of you who are consumed by a stronger and less satisfied thirst than the thirst tormenting others: Seize for yourselves, the larger share that is coming to you! Cease believing yourselves to be the disinherited children of the heavenly Father. He will not stand for you being anything other than his privileged children, those most "conformed to the image of his Son" (Romans 8:29). With greater faith and love, you will find that not one of your bitter trials fails to offer an anticipated fulfillment.

Here is a poor servant of Jesus Christ, confined for years to a bed of inactivity and pain, who sees days of suffering end only to be replaced by nights of insomnia. Very well, that is God's chosen means for more fully satisfying his thirst. With a healthy body and an easy life he would have been spared many troubles, but he would also have lost precious opportunities to prepare himself—I should have said, to be prepared—through trials, through patience, through prayer, perhaps even through contrast, to more keenly sense a deeper bliss. "Behold, we count them blessed who have suffered" (see James 5:11); and those who suffer today will tomorrow be those who have suffered. Ah, my brother, will you complain today of that which tomorrow will be "your strength and your song" (see Psalm 118:14)?[3]

And you, my sister, who are inwardly consumed by the sweet and powerful need to love and be loved, none has appreciated the consolations of the family hearth better than you. Having been refused those consolations, you find yourself to be "lonely and afflicted" (Psalm 25:16). Refused, but by whom? By blind fate? No, but by a fatherly providence. And why? In order to deprive you of that which is lavished on others? No, but to enrich you more than anyone else. Believe it well, "God has provided something better for [you]" (Hebrews 11:40) in reducing you to seek your fullness in his love and to confine all the most legitimate, most noble, most inalienable desires of your being to him alone. If you were to have that family life that you have so longed for, perhaps even envied, you would gain the joys that you lack, that's true—and whoever knows how to love will also grant that the sweetness of those joys is undiminished by the pains associated with them—but you would also lose a merciful discipline that is designed to train you through unreserved renouncement for an undivided love.

---

[3] Perhaps some readers are thinking here, "Easy for Monod to say when he is healthy." It is worth noting, however, (and those who have read *Living in the Hope of Glory* will know) that over the last two years of his life, and particularly over the last six months, Monod was suffering intensely from liver cancer, yet his views remained constant. He found peace and even joy in the midst of his pain.

Each of you, "men of sorrows" (see Isaiah 53:3)—destitute, sick, sad, abandoned—what do you have to complain of? Of being placed among the ranks of those blessed who weep (Luke 6:21), of the poor who are the richest of all, of the weak who are the strongest of all? Listen to me—or rather, listen to yourselves. Would you like this very hour to change places with those who are favored by life? Try to beseech God with your whole heart, as Jabez did, "Oh . . . that you would keep me from harm so that it might not bring me pain!" (1 Chronicles 4:10). Who knows, perhaps through perseverance your prayer will be granted, just as his was. . . . But no, you wouldn't dare to pray like that. Unlike you, Jabez didn't know the gospel and, unlike you, he had not received the Holy Spirit. The depth of your heart is in such agreement with me—or, rather, with Jesus Christ!—that you would tremble at the thought of withdrawing from those trials arranged for you by a Father who "does not willingly afflict or grieve the children of men" (Lamentations 3:33).

Courage, then, dear children, favored children, marked as such by the thirst that devours you! (see Ezekiel 9:4). With Jesus' faith, fix your eyes on "the joy that is set before you" (see Hebrews 12:2), and in Jesus' Spirit, bless all those pains that open the way for you, even as, with freedom, love and happiness, you gather the least little flower, no matter how lonely or small, that God causes to spring up under your feet in your valley of tears. Thus you will relive the amazing experiences that the Judean wilderness brought about for David in the wilderness of his own heart. Having begun by crying out with him, "My soul thirsts for you; my flesh faints for you, as in a dry and weary land where there is no water" (Psalm 63:1), you will find in the divine life something greater than all the ills of human life and greater than all its good things: "Your steadfast love is better than life" (Psalm 63:3). Then you will end up breaking into triumphant song, almost in spite of yourself and of all that surrounds you, and singing,

"My soul will be satisfied as with fat and rich food, and my mouth will praise you with joyful lips" (Psalm 63:5). Thus, anticipating the day when the angel of the Apocalypse will invite you to drink from Jesus' hand the cup of his heavenly joy (see Revelation 21:6), you will drink avidly from this same Jesus' hand the cup of his earthly bitterness: "If anyone thirsts, let him come to me and drink!"

Quenching the Thirst of Others

Are you able to receive a still higher comfort, one that is purely of love and is found in the satisfaction not of your own thirst but of the thirst of others? No, the word comfort is too weak in this context. The term glory is far more appropriate. What could be more glorious than to enter not only into the spirit of Jesus Christ but into his very work; to be, in some sense, crucified for your fellows? Let me hasten to explain.

Jesus Saving Others

The fruit that Jesus was to gather for himself from his abasement and sacrifice was not the unique source of the peace that he knew in the midst of suffering. It was not even the dominant source. Jesus always gave preeminence to love. After the glory of his Father, whose name he came to reveal to men, what preoccupied him the most was the salvation of those whom the Father had given him out of the world (John 17:6). Without them it seemed that neither his glory nor his bliss could be complete: "Father, I desire that they also, whom you have given me, may be with me where I am, to see my glory that you have given me" (John 17:24).

The mysterious thirst that we have recognized in him— a thirst for his baptism of bitterness, for his farewell Passover, for the cup of Gethsemane, and for the sacrifice of

Golgotha—all this blends itself into a thirst for the fulfillment of those who are his. Do not doubt this. Who can tell what part we had even in his last cry of anguish, "I thirst" (John 19:28), which is immediately followed by his last word of peace, "It is finished" (John 19:30)? A day will come when all will be finished in glory, just as then it was finished in suffering; a day when the first use Jesus will make of that new glory will be to offer eternal fulfillment for the thirst of those who are his. "It is done! I am the Alpha and the Omega, the beginning and the end. To the thirsty I will give from the spring of the water of life without payment" (Revelation 21:6).[4] There is no cost to us, but think what it cost him! Never mind; a heart such as his tastes on the cross a kind of bitter sweetness through the awareness that he suffers only that which saves us and experiences only those torments from which he thus spares those whom he redeems!

Leading the Thirsty to the Savior

Away, away with all thought of participating in Jesus' atoning work! On this ground, reserved for the only Son of God, what man, what angel, what created being would dare to venture except through folly and ungodliness? But if we cannot suffer in order to save men, we can at least suffer in order to lead them to the Savior; and it is a glorious enough thing for unworthy sinners such as we to be crucified for the sake of their brothers. Saint Paul in no wise disdained it. Rather, he was almost beside himself with joy when, in thus associating his pain with that of his Master, he uttered these astonishing—I was going to say foolhardy—words: "I rejoice

---

[4] This comparison is full of instruction. Having come to the final stage of his suffering, Jesus says, "I thirst; it is finished;" having come to the highest stage of his glory, Jesus says, "It is done, let him who is thirsty come to me." And it is the same Saint John who retraces both scenes for us. [A.M.]

in my sufferings for your sake, and in my flesh I am filling up what is lacking in Christ's afflictions for the sake of his body, that is, the church" (Colossians 1:24). A true minister of Jesus Christ, a true servant of the church, Saint Paul succeeds in exhausting that which his Master might have left unexplored in the field of human suffering. He finds abundant consolation, not to mention superabundant joy, in the thought that all he endures serves "for the perfecting of the saints . . . for the edifying of the body of Christ" (Ephesians 4:12 KJV).

Very well, that consolation, that vibrant joy of both sorrow and love is what Jesus offers you in my text. Confident in your love, he has only just promised to satisfy your thirst in him—"If anyone thirsts, let him come to me and drink" (John 7:37)—when he goes on to promise you that you yourselves will satisfy the thirst of others— "Whoever believes in me, . . . out of his heart will flow rivers of living water" (John 7:38). Once already he had made the same promises related to one another in the same way: "Whoever drinks of the water that I will give him will never be thirsty forever. The water that I will give him will become in him a spring of water welling up to eternal life" (John 4:14). These are tender words that our evangelist-turned-prophet will later show us to be fulfilled in the touching scene that concludes the book of Revelation. Whoever has heard the invitation of the Spirit and the Bride saying "Come" will likewise say "Come" to those who have not yet done so; and none will ascend to the fountain of life who does not hold out his hand to those who follow him, causing them, in turn, to ascend.

Is this not, at a different level, the same sentiment that inspires Saint Paul as he exhorts, "Let the thief no longer steal, but rather let him labor, doing honest work with his own hands, so that he may have something to share with anyone in need" (Ephesians 4:28). In nature as in grace, "it is more blessed to give than to receive" (Acts 20:35), and it is the nature of gospel love to savor nothing so much in the pleasure of receiving as the ability to give.

Sharing Our Fulfillment

Jesus' satisfied thirst has taught you to seek in him the spiritual life that is designed to satisfy your thirst. Now may your own satisfied thirst give the same lesson to others, not in order to lead them to you, but in order to lead them to the one who has satisfied you and who will, in turn, satisfy them as they come to him in faith. You should especially note that this lesson will be all the more persuasive when your thirst has been more consuming and your fulfillment has been more difficult to obtain.

Perhaps you are among those whom God seems to have chosen to be an example of a thirst that nothing is able to extinguish. Perhaps you have seen all the things that made up "the delight of your eyes" (Ezekiel 24:21) fall at your side, one after another, leaving you in the end to dwell alone on earth. Perhaps a somber melancholy, having taken hold of you at the beginning of your career, has gnawed at your heart, paralyzed your strength, ruined your plans, and troubled your entire life. Finally, perhaps "your pain is unceasing and your wound incurable, refusing to be healed" (see Jeremiah 15:18). When in such circumstances your thirst is quenched—as it can be, as it must be, as it will be if you are faithful—this will clearly demonstrate that with Jesus Christ we need never despair.

Suppose there should appear on life's stage another parched person who "passes through waterless places seeking rest, but finds none" (Matthew 12:43). After long and fruitless effort, he is ready to "grow weary or fainthearted" (Hebrews 12:3). He has not yet begun to know the name of the Lord, but another name is placed between him and despair: your name. In observing you, he will say to himself,

"That man has been as parched as I am. What outward affliction, what inward heaviness has he lacked? What tears has he not shed? What battles has he not had to wage? How many times has he not been tempted to believe that all was lost? And yet, here he is delivered, content, serene. Why shouldn't I arrive at the same result if I take the same path?"

If he says this and if he does what he says, will you not have been for this unfortunate person, as nearly as possible, that which Jesus Christ has been for you? Will you not have been, in some human measure, "crucified" for him?

I don't know what this supposition says to your heart, but it causes mine to tremble. Place a "man of sorrows" (Isaiah 53:3) here in this pulpit in my place and in front of this text; a man to whom a deep sadness has given a more than ordinary need to lay hold of Jesus Christ through a more than ordinary sense of the void in the human heart; a man who has been doubly prepared by a long career of bitterness to speak to you of thirst and fulfillment, making his discourses more piercing when he describes the one and his example more persuasive when he savors the other; a man who was chosen by God to serve as a sign to his brothers, as Ezekiel once did (see Ezekiel 24:16-24), through the wounds of his soul and the battles of his life. Can you imagine the touching anointing with which such a man would appeal to your hearts? And when he had gained one of you to Jesus Christ, how much lighter would he not find his cross to be, in discovering that God had given it to him to carry for you?

Freely Receiving to Freely Give

You parched and thirsty souls, finish quenching the thirst that devours you through the hope of quenching the thirst of others! Come, and may it be learned from you that there is nobody whose thirst Jesus cannot satisfy since he has satisfied even yours! Come, and may all your suffering, felt but assuaged, instruct those who surround you with regard to both the needs that are in man and the riches that are in God! Come, and if God has placed you in the ranks of those crucified ones whom he desires to make a visible type of thirst and fulfillment, let yourself be crucified with abandon, with joy, and with love! Being in turn both satisfied and satisfying, "having received without paying" in order to "give without pay" (Matthew 10:8), come extinguish in the cup of Jesus' love the remnant of thirst that his cup of life and his cup of bitterness have left to you. "If anyone thirsts, let him come to me and drink!" [5]

---

[5] A section relating particularly to mid-19th century France, "The Thirst of Our Age" has been omitted here.

part two
BEHOLD YOUR GOD

(Isaiah 40:9)

part two

A stranger intruding on holy ground—that's exactly how I felt the first time I had occasion to write the name Jesus after becoming a believer. Of course, I wasn't a stranger. I had met the Lord Jesus and committed myself to him. Yet I still knew very little about him. For each of us, entering into a relationship of love and trust with God through Jesus Christ is only the beginning. As with any relationship, we must learn over time to know our loved one better. And so I set out on an adventure of discovery that is still going on today. In that adventure, Adolphe Monod's writings and sermons have, for over two decades, been a wonderful guide and a source of inspiration and strength. The three sermons in this section illumine three essential aspects of God's nature.

"God is Love" was written and preached for those who are familiar—too familiar—with the marvelous story of God's love seen in our redemption. When we first meet God, the wonder of this miracle of grace is fresh on our hearts. Over the years, as we hear it again and again, much of that freshness can be lost, and it is easy to lose the fire of our first love for God. The clear logic, beautiful imagery, and powerful insights of this message are designed to rekindle that love.

In "I Am the Resurrection and the Life," an Easter sermon, Monod gives a wonderful perspective on the nature of Jesus' resurrection and of ours. Eternal life is not something that is awaiting us in heaven. It begins here on earth when we commit ourselves to God and have Christ's life placed within us.

Finally, "Too Late!" is the sermon that Monod really didn't like preaching. It deals with God's faithfulness in his warnings and threats as well as in his promises. Like Monod, evangelical Christianity today generally prefers to emphasize

God's love and forgiveness, but God is holy as well as loving. He cannot ignore sin. Thus, his stern warnings have the loving goal of leading us to repentance, and we must learn to take them seriously, not only for ourselves but also to motivate us for reaching the unconverted with the gospel.

— *CHW*

God Is Love

☙

(Montauban, 1843)

1 John 4:7-9

Dear friends, let us love one another, for love is from God, and whoever loves has been born of God and knows God. Anyone who does not love does not know God, because God is love. In this the love of God was made manifest among us, that God sent his only Son into the world, so that we might live through him.

The Hidden Word

A small village in Italy was buried eighteen hundred years ago under a river of lava from the Mount Vesuvius volcano. There ancient burned manuscripts have been found that resemble lumps of charcoal more than books. Using ingenious methods, they are being slowly and painfully unrolled, line by line, word by word. Let's suppose that one of these scrolls from Herculanum contains a copy of our epistle; the only copy in the world. Arriving at the fourth chapter and the eighth verse, the two words "God is" have just been deciphered, while the word that follows is still unknown. What suspense! That which philosophers have sought so long in vain, that which the wisest among them have finally given up hope of discovering, a definition of God—here it is and here it is from the hand of God himself. God is . . . What will we be told, and what is he?

The Question of Questions

What is he, this hidden God, "who dwells in unapproachable light, whom no one has ever seen or can see" (1 Timothy 6:16)? "We seek God, in the hope that we might feel our way toward him. . . . Yet he is actually not far from each one of us" (see Acts 17:27). He constrains us to cry out with Job, "Oh, that I knew where I might find him . . . ! Behold, I go forward, but he is not there, and backward, but I do not perceive him; on the left hand when he is working, I do not behold him; he turns to the right hand, but I do not see him" (Job 23:3,8-9).

What is he, this mighty God, who created all that is with a single word, and who can destroy it with another word? "For in him we live and move and have our being" (Acts 17:28). He holds us under his hand every moment, and he can do what he pleases with us—with our existence, with our circumstances, with our home, with our society, with our body, and with our spirit itself.

Finally, what is he, this holy God, who is "of purer eyes than to see evil" (Habakkuk 1:13)? Our consciences convince us of having offended him, and nature vaguely reveals to us his anger, yet neither conscience nor nature gives us any indication of whether there is pardon with him. This is the just judge into whose hands we are going to fall when we leave here—perhaps tomorrow, perhaps today—having no idea of the eternal sentence that he reserves for us and knowing only that we have merited that the verdict should be against us.

What is he? Our rest, our salvation, our eternity—all are at stake, and I seem to see all of God's creatures leaning over the holy book, waiting in solemn silence for what it will reveal to the world about the question of questions.

The Best Possible Answer

Look, the fateful word is discovered: *love.* "God is love." What better answer could we desire? Of what comparable thing could the boldest, most confident imagination conceive? This hidden God, this mighty God, this holy God—he is love. What more do we need? God loves us. No, more than that; everything in God is love. Love is the very essence of God. He who says "God" says "love." "God is love!" Oh, answer that surpasses all of our hopes! Oh, blessed revelation that puts an end to all of our anxieties! Oh, certain pledge of our bliss—present, future, and eternal!

Yes, all this is true for us, but only if we can believe; for it is not enough for God to be love if we cannot say with Saint John, "We have come to know and to believe the love that God has for us" (1 John 4:16). God's love can neither console us nor enlighten us nor sanctify us nor even save us—God's love is, for us, as if it didn't exist—just as long as it has not been "poured into our hearts through the Holy Spirit" (Romans 5:5), and "united with us by faith" (see Hebrews 4:2).[1] As spiritual and responsible creatures, we have the glorious but terrible privilege of being able to open ourselves or close ourselves to God's love. Thus, we either take advantage of or exclude ourselves from that love, which is the treasure of the human race and the hope of the universe. Faith in God's love, then, is the sentiment that I would like to inspire in each of you. Oh, if I could send you

---

[1] Through faith, God's Word penetrates our souls and is united with them, just as food which enters our bodies is assimilated into their substance. [A.M.]

forth from here moved, gripped, penetrated by the thought: "God is love!"

Lord, if it is true that you are love, make it known by guiding my tongue with your love and by opening the hearts of everyone here to that love.

Love Gives Itself

True love does not simply declare itself, it reveals itself; or better yet, according to a lovely expression of Saint John, it gives itself (see 1 John 3:1). Thus God is not content with telling us that he is love; he proves it to us through visible signs and striking deeds that transform this touching doctrine into an even more touching story. Open your ears and listen; open your eyes and see. Nothing more is needed for you to recognize that God is love.

Love Inherent in Creation

The deeds I will cite are not borrowed from creation or our natural life. To be sure, both are filled with God's love, for "the LORD is good to all" (Psalm 145:9), and "everything that has breath praises the LORD" (see Psalm 150:6). Yet the proofs that creation and natural life furnish would be insufficient to persuade us that God is love, because marks of anger are united with marks of love in the work of the Creator God.

It is true, however, that if we were to take the trouble to untangle these contradictory witnesses, in order to separate the Creator's part from that of the creature, we would find that the marks of anger in no way entered into the plan of creation. God's work as it went forth from his hands—and as he was anxious for man to leave it—shone forth love as the sun shines forth light.

What love there is in the work of those six days, each of which, in Moses' account, ends with the words, "And God saw that it was good," while the last ends with, "And God saw everything that he had made, and behold, it was very good" (Genesis 1:31)!

What love there is in that light of the heavens, in that fruitful earth, in that ordering of the seasons, in those torches of the firmament, in that living multitude that populates and animates all of creation!

What love there is in that man, made in God's image; able to think, to speak and to love. Reflect on it, what love there is in that phrase, "Let us make man in our image, after our likeness" (Genesis 1:26)!

What love there is in that Eden—that is to say, that place of delights—and in man's week divided between such easy work and such sweet repose, in imitation of God's own week!

What love there is in that woman formed from Adam's rib, in that union at once so tender and so pure, and in that innocent bliss which, all unknown as it is to us, has left a vague and painful memory in the depths of our hearts!

What love there is in that tree of the knowledge of good and evil by which God tested our first parents and which, had they been faithful, was supposed to exchange their childish innocence for a thoughtful and free obedience.

Ah, you may be sure that if we had been able to question Adam before his fall, we would have heard the exclamation of our text coming forth out of the abundance of his heart, and we would have read it in each of his glances: "God is love."

A Higher but Too Familiar Love

But I want to speak to you of another love, a love with which God loves you today and loves you just as you are. I want to make you see this love concentrated in an act; in a single act that sufficed for our apostle and that will equally suffice for us if we can meditate on it. Saint John, himself, goes on to develop his thought: "In this the love of God was made manifest among us, that God sent his only Son into the world, so that we might live through him. In this is love, not that we have loved God but that he loved us and sent his Son to be the propitiation for our sins." (1 John 4:9-10).

Yet as I open up this doctrine in order to show you the treasure of love that it enfolds, a secret fear restrains and troubles me. I know that there is a marvel of love here, capable of astonishing, confounding, and delighting us, but I fear I will be heard coldly. Alas, if I must tell all my thoughts, I fear that I might speak coldly of it myself. Just as the daily contemplation of nature has made us almost insensitive to the beauties with which it sparkles, so the habit of hearing the gospel has dulled us to this ineffable gift which all the powers of our soul are incapable of sensing and worthily celebrating.

In order to arouse the attention of his readers, a philosopher of antiquity, describing the marvels of creation, imagines that they are presented for the first time to the gaze of a man who has spent his entire life in a dark cave, and he seeks the impressions that such a sight would produce on such an observer. I want to do something similar with you. Let us ask what effect the gospel—that is to say, the good news—would produce on the soul of a pagan hearing it for the first time after spending his whole life, up to this point, in the spiritual darkness of gross idolatry.

Better than that, let us leave hypothesis aside and take a historical event. The Moravian missionaries who carried the gospel to Greenland thought that they had to prepare the spirits of the natives to receive it by speaking to them at first only of the general truths of religion: the existence of God, the obedience required by his laws, and a future reward. This went on for several years, during which time they saw no fruit from their labors. Finally, one day, they decided to risk speaking to them of the Savior and reading to them the account of his passion. They had no sooner finished than one of their listeners, a man named Kajarnak, approached the table where missionary Beck was seated and said to him in a strong but emotional voice, "What did you just say? Repeat that for us. I, too, want to be saved!" [2] Kajarnak believed, lived as a Christian, and died in peace, the blessed first fruits of an abundant harvest.

Very well, let us put ourselves in the place of that pagan whose conscience has just been awakened, and let us seek to explain to ourselves the vivid impression he gets of this gospel that is completely new to him. In order to do so, we need only follow our apostle, step by step, in the very brief but also very full description that we just read to you. There we see, all at once, that sinful man can again have a share in eternal life, that God sent his Son into the world, clothed in mortal flesh, that he delivered him up to death as an atonement for our sins, and that he did all of that for us freely, when we had merited only his wrath.

Love's Goal

The first thing that would cause Kajarnak to recognize that God is love is *the goal* God sets for himself in the gospel and that the apostle expresses in the words, "that we might live" (1 John 4:9). Though the sinner might have merited death a thousand times, God's desire is not that he should die but that he should live. He has declared it and he has sworn it by himself, "As surely as I live, declares the Lord GOD, I have no pleasure in the death of the wicked, but that the

---

[2] Cranz, *Geshichte von Groenland*, p 490 [A.M.; the full citation is, David Cranz, *Fortsetzung der Historie von Grönland : insonderheit der Missions-Geschichte der Evangelischen Brüder zu Neu-Herrnhut und Lichtenfels von 1763 bis 1768* (In commission bey Weidmanns Erben und Reich, 1770)].

wicked turn from his way and live" (Ezekiel 33:11). The more that the life God wants to give the sinner is explained to Kajarnak; the more he is surprised, charmed, moved by such a love.

That We Might Live

The life God wants to give is the life of grace. It is the pardon of all our offenses—a pardon that erases, that removes sin. "To remove my sin," this simple man says to himself, "what language! When I have dirtied my hands with the blood of my enemy, I remove it with water from the sea or with the snow of heaven, but to remove sin from my conscience and give me back the peace that I had before committing it—what grace, what love!"

That life is the life of heaven. It is possessing God's glory in the resting place of the blessed and in the company of the holy angels. "A sinner such as I, called to such glory, admitted to such a resting place, received into such a society—what a calling, what love!"

That life is the life of God. It is God's Spirit, it is God himself coming to dwell within the sinner. It is God giving himself to him, uniting himself with him—isn't that the distinctive feature of love? "God making his abode in my soul as in a favorite sanctuary; in this soul that seemed to be reserved only for the demon and his angels—what condescension, what love!

"But that news, that excellent news, is it really true? Can it be true? What about God's law that I have broken? What about God's Word, pledged to punish sin with death? What about God's justice, concerned with punishing my crimes? What becomes of those?"

The Marvel of Grace

Perhaps it seems to many of you that I am attributing unnatural thoughts to Kajarnak. You find nothing to astonish you in this pardon from God in which he can scarcely believe. You who are saturated with knowledge of the gospel without having received the gospel in your hearts, instead of a marvelous grace you can see only a simple thing that God owes to his creatures and owes to himself. "Is it really such a grand affair to pardon? Isn't that the noblest use a ruler can make of his power? And how could those perfections that we attribute to God lead us to expect anything less from him? No doubt we are sinners, but 'for every sin there is mercy.' " That is one of those popular sayings in which, by a frightful confusion of truth and error, the gospel is used to nullify the gospel.

"For every sin there is mercy." True saying, holy saying, divine saying if you say it with surprise and rapture, as something almost unbelievable: "Then it really is true that there is a pardon for all our sins!" But false saying, saying of sin, saying of perdition when you say it without joy, without emotion, as something that follows completely naturally from God's perfections and man's miseries: "For every sin there is mercy." Ah, the trouble is that you judge God by your own standard.

For you, "brought forth in iniquity and conceived in sin" (see Psalm 51:5), it is a simple thing to tolerate in others, without indignation and without surprise, that which has become second nature in you. But is it the same for this God whose is "of purer eyes than to see evil" (Habakkuk 1:13), who "will by no means clear the guilty" (Numbers 14:18), and who has pronounced death and a curse against whoever transgresses his commandments? It must not be, it cannot be that his Word should be found vain, or his law be trampled under foot, or his justice be disarmed. God would not be God if he pardoned in the way that you intend. You need to realize that there is an obstacle on the path of this pardon, an immense obstacle, an obstacle that is forever insurmountable for anyone other than the one for whom "nothing will be impossible" (Luke 1:37).

Reconciling Mercy with Justice

Far from going beyond the truth, the thoughts that we have attributed to Kajarnak remain well below it. Kajarnak is still too unenlightened as to the divine perfections really to appreciate the problem. The more he increases in light, the more he will see the problem grow before him. But give it to those who are more advanced to resolve.

Give it to that sinner who has long been weary and burdened, who is so touched by his misery and by God's holiness that he cannot persuade himself that there is a pardon for him. Give it to him to resolve and you will hear him praying in his inner closet, "Forgive me, oh my God, if you can forgive me without doing violence to your holy law!"

Give it to that profound theologian who labors night and day in the contemplation of grace, and you will see him writing in a journal where he confides his most secret thoughts, "I would not want a salvation in which the law is not honored and my sin removed."[3]

Better still, give it to the angels of heaven. Place yourselves with them between the fall and the promise, and ask them how God might be able to pardon without ceasing to be just; ask them how he could show grace to the sinner without sparing sin.

Come, heavenly spirits, learned in sublime meditations, you who have penetrated so deeply into the thoughts of divine love; try to resolve this great problem. Gather up all the strength of your immortal spirits. Summon all the philosophy from on high to your aid. Search, meditate, climb to the third heaven, go down into the deepest depths, and tell us, if you know, a means of pardoning without ceasing to be just and of showing grace to the sinner without sparing sin.

---

[3] *Memoir of Griffin*, by Sprague, p 27 [A.M.; the full citation is *Memoir of the Rev. Edward D. Griffin, D.D., compiled chiefly from his own writings*, by William Buehl Sprague, New York, Taylor & Dodd, 1839, p 27]

But how could you angels have discovered something that, once revealed, astonishes and overwhelms your reason? How could you anticipate God's thinking in the gospel—you whom the Holy Spirit portrays to us as bent down over this thought just as the cherubim are bent over the ark, never able to satisfy "the longing" that consumes you "to look into these things" (see 1 Peter 1:12). Ah, it is better to keep silent and to listen with us to the voice of God himself coming out of heaven: "I have found a ransom" (Job 33:24).

He has found it, and this success is such an astounding marvel, requiring the involvement of all the fullness of his deity, that he even seems to astound himself at having discovered it. He has found it, but he has found it completely within his own bosom. "His own arm brought him salvation, and his righteousness upheld him" (Isaiah 59:16). All this work is "from him and through him and to him" (Romans 11:36). He has found it. "Glory to God in the highest, and on earth peace among those with whom he is pleased" (Luke 2:14). This God who has found the propitiation, this God who has wanted so much to give us life that he seemingly triumphed over his righteousness and his law—is this God not love?

Love's Method

If the goal God has proposed for himself in our redemption touches Kajarnak's heart, the *means* he has used to redeem us touches it still more. God has found the propitiation, and here is the propitiation he has found: He sent his only Son into the world (John 3:16-17).

God Has a Son

God has a Son! What astounding news! Accustomed as we are from birth to hearing about this Son of God, we fail to sense all that is foreign in that single idea of paternity, of generation, associated with the name of the Creator God. Kajarnak is struck far more forcefully by it than we are; but the pious missionary scarcely rests his attention on these depths. Anxious to speak to Kajarnak's heart, he touches on this mystery only as much as is necessary to give him some idea of the inconceivable love that must unite this Father to this Son.

Just the name of Son already reveals it, for what more tender name could the Holy Spirit choose when he wanted to give us some picture of that eternal love through an earthly relationship? But that is not enough for him. To this name of Son he joins others that elevate it still further. This is "God's only Son," "his own Son," "his beloved Son" (see John 3:16, Romans 8:3, Matthew 3:17). This is his only Son, the one who maintains a relationship with him in which no creature can participate. It is his own Son, who belongs to him in truth, who is really and not figuratively born from him. It is his beloved Son, "with whom [he is] well pleased" (Matthew 3:17).

Oh, what a combination of strength and simplicity there is in the words, "The Father loves the Son!" He loves him and communicates all his power to him: "The Father loves the Son and has given all things into his hand" (John 3:35). He loves him and shares all his secrets with him: "The Father loves the Son and shows him all that he himself is doing" (John 5:20). He loves him from all eternity: "Father . . . you loved me before the foundation of the world" (John 17:24). He loves him, and that love of the Father for the Son is the eternal type of all true love. All other love is merely a reflection of it, and the most wonderful thing that the Son can ask for his dearest disciples is that "the Father might love them as he has loved me" (see John 17:23).

Oh, who will say what this Son is for this Father? Who will tell us of those intimate outpourings of sentiment, that inexpressible tenderness, that eternal dwelling of the Son in the bosom of the Father? Who will spread out before our eyes all the meaning of this phrase: "I was daily his delight, rejoicing before him always" (Proverbs 8:30)?

Given for Us

Very well, how will Kajarnak feel on learning that this Son of God, this only Son, this beloved Son is the one whom the Father sends into the world, the one whom he distances from his throne, from his glory, and from his bosom in order that we might live through him! If God's Son is so great, so precious, so dear to his eyes, then what are we to him—we for whom he has given this so great, so precious, so dear Son?

If a captain ransoms his prisoners who are held by the enemy at the price of gold, isn't it because the freedom of his companions is just as dear to him and even more dear than the gold with which he redeems them? If Abraham offers his son Isaac as a burnt offering, isn't it because God's holy will is just as dear to him and even more dear than the life of this son whom he loves so much? If God "gives men in return for Israel, peoples in exchange for his life" (see Isaiah 43:4), isn't it because Israel is just as dear to him and even more dear than the men, the peoples whom he gives for their deliverance?

And if, given the alternative of either striking us while sparing his only Son or delivering up his only Son in order to spare us, the Father delivers up his Son and spares us, what can we say about the love with which he loves us? What can we say that would not appear to be the epitome of waywardness and presumption if we did not have the truth, the evidence, the very revelation of God on our side? Whatever the case, he delivers him up, he gives him, he sends him into the world—into this world that is lost through sin but, for that very reason, needs him in order to be saved.

In the Likeness of Sinful Flesh

The Father does still more. He sends his Son here in the form of sinful man, "in the likeness of sinful flesh" (Romans 8:3). For Saint Paul tells us, "he had to be made like his brothers in every respect" (Hebrews 2:17), and "since, therefore the children share in flesh and blood, he himself likewise partook of the same things, that through death he might destroy the one who has the power of death, that is, the devil" (Hebrews 2:14).

Have you ever reflected on this, my dear brothers? What an honor for our nature, for this poor fallen nature, that the Father should clothe the Son with it—the Son who is "the radiance of the glory of God and the exact imprint of his nature" (Hebrews 1:3), the Son who "was in the form of God . . . but made himself nothing, taking the form of a servant, being born in likeness of men" (Philippians 2:6-7)! But also what abasement for the Son, what a marvel of condescension and love on the part of the Father who gave him!

What was it like for the "King of kings and Lord of lords" (1 Timothy 6:15) to be born of a woman and to fall from the womb of his creature onto an accursed earth? What was it like for "the Son of the Most High" (Luke 1:32) to exchange the bosom of the Father for a dwelling place of which Satan is called the prince? What was it like for "the LORD, strong and mighty" (Psalm 24:8) to endure toil, weariness, and pain? Or for the one whom "angels worship" (Hebrews 1:6) to drag around a body of dust and mud? Or for "the Lord of glory" (1 Corinthians 2:8) to see himself subjected to the weaknesses and humiliations of the flesh? Or for the "heir of all things" (Hebrews 1:2) to support a perishable body with perishable food? Or for "the most Holy" One (Daniel 9:24 KJV) to be tempted by the Devil? Or for "the Author of life" (Acts 3:15) to undergo the degradation of death and the tomb?

Then, too, consider the astounding thought that this mystery inspires in Saint Paul. What the Lord does for us here, he does for us alone. He has done nothing similar for the angels. "For surely," says the apostle, "it is not angels that he helps, but he helps the offspring of Abraham" (Hebrews 2:16). Oh, what love to have conceived the idea of associating the very Son of God with our misery in order to draw us out of it! The God who sent his Son into the world in order that we might live through him—is this God not love?

Love's Task

But with what message did the Father charge the Son, and what *work* did he give him to do in sending him into the world? He "sent his Son," answers the apostle, "to be the propitiation for our sins" (1 John 4:10), and the work he was given to do was the atonement for our crimes through his blood.

To Bear Our Punishment

Atonement: a commonplace word among us, a well-worn doctrine that a child knows by heart; but what a word, what a doctrine for Beck's student of Christianity![4] You just heard, Kajarnak, that God sent his Son into the world in order to save you. Now listen to how he must save you. This "Holy and Righteous One" (Acts 3:14) must take your place and receive the blow that you have earned but that the Father wants to divert from you. "All we like sheep have gone astray," far from God and from his law; "and the LORD has laid on him the iniquity of us all" (Isaiah 53:6), mine and yours—do you hear it well? And then "he was wounded for

---

[4] "Student of Christianity" here is literally "catechumen," one studying the catechism in preparation for acceptance into full church membership.

our transgressions; he was crushed for our iniquities; upon him was the chastisement that brought us peace, and with his stripes we are healed" (Isaiah 53:5). Listen again: "For our sake, [God] made him to be sin who knew no sin, so that in him we might become the righteousness of God" (2 Corinthians 5:21).

What do you say to this, Kajarnak? Did you foresee it, would you have imagined it, would you have dreamed of it—that an offended God would shed the blood of his own Son in order to wash away your offenses? In distant and privileged countries from which this astonishing news was brought to you, I could show you men, entire assemblies of men who find this to be quite simple and ordinary. But you, though they may charge you with exaggeration and enthusiasm, what do you say? What could you say?

A Cruel Death at Satan's Hand

But come, follow me to the foot of the cross of God's Son. That is a sight that demands closer contemplation. The "hour" is come, "and the power of darkness" (Luke 22:53); the hour whose mere approach causes him such cruel agony that a sweat of blood comes out of his body and flows down to form deposits on the ground. But this is also the hour from which the Father could not spare him, if he wanted to spare us.

Abraham, as he is ready to carry out his sacrifice, hears the voice of an angel crying out to him, "Abraham, Abraham! . . . Do not lay your hand on the boy" (Genesis 22:11-12), but this other Abraham has no one above him to restrain his arm as it is ready to strike. What God did not require of his servant, he demands of himself, and he won't stop until the sacrifice has been completed.

Come rage of hell, come fury of earth, come wrath of heaven; empty out all the most formidable things you possess on that innocent head which the Lord has abandoned to your power, and "do whatever [his] hand and [his] plan had predestined to take place" (Acts 4:28)!

Satan, "that ancient serpent" (Revelation 12:9), impatient to fulfill the first prophesy, lifts his hideous head and hisses as he bruises the heel of the offspring of the woman (see Genesis 3:15). Recently defeated by the one he had come to tempt, he withdrew for a time, but now the Father allows him to come back and to raise up his entire army against the Son. He allows him to enter into Judas so that he will betray him, into Caiaphas so that he will condemn him, and into Pilate so that he will deliver him up for punishment. If Satan was unable to make the Holy One fall in the desert, he will be able to make the Prince of Life die on Golgotha. He is granted this victory so that "through death he [Jesus] might . . . deliver all those who through fear of death were subject to lifelong slavery" (Hebrews 2:14-15).

Rejected by Men

Here is something still more shocking. That this formidable angel, the eternal enemy of God and men, should set himself against the Son of God and the Savior of men is unworthy, but it can at least be conceived. What about those men he came to save, those men whose nature he has put on? The Father delivered him into their hands, and how do they treat him? "They . . . do to him whatever they please" (see Matthew 17:12). It is not just that they don't treat him as the Son of God; it is not just that they don't treat him as a king or as a prophet or as a righteous person. They don't treat him as a man. They, the worms of this earth, reduce him, the Son of God, to cry out under the weight of their hatred and disdain, "I am a worm and not a man, scorned by mankind and despised by the people" (Psalm 22:6)!

They sell him one to another. They value him at the price of thirty pieces of silver at the very moment when he values them at the price of his own blood. They surprise him by night, armed with swords and clubs. They tie him up, dragging him from Pilate to Herod and from Herod to Pilate. They mock him as king, robing him in scarlet and crowning him with thorns. They mock him as prophet, hitting him and saying, "Prophesy! Who is it that struck you?" (Luke 22:64). They mock him as the Son of God, crying out to him, "Are you not the Christ? Save yourself!" (Luke 23:39).

They strike him with a whip, they spit in his face, they condemn him to death, they choose Barabbas over him. They crucify him with a criminal on his right and another on his left. And while even the worst scoundrels, at least in this supreme moment, excite more pity than anger, even amongst their cruelest enemies, for him alone has the Father reserved the dreadful privilege of arousing the laughter, the irony, the sarcasm of his persecutors! He arouses them on his cross; he arouses them in his agony; he arouses them with his cries and with his prayers.

Abandoned by the Father

That's still not all. In fact, that is small compared to what is left to say. To whom? To you? No, but to Kajarnak, to a pagan who fortunately isn't familiar with these things, or at least isn't familiar with them the way you are. You know the sufferings of your Savior as one knows the fables of Homer or the stories of earlier ages.

When the Son was alone—alone in the temptation in the wilderness, alone in the agony of Gethsemane, alone on the cross—he could say, "I am not alone, for my Father is with me" (John 16:32). But what would it be like if the Father himself were to abandon him? The rage of the demon, the hatred of the Pharisees, the cries of the populace, the cowardice of Pilate, the sarcasm of the priests—against all of these, God, his God, his Father sustained and consoled him; but who will console him, who will sustain him against the wrath, against the curse, against the terrible justice of God himself?

That death, that torture, that broken body, that shed blood, those insults are, without doubt, bitter aspects of the cross. But the real bitterness lies elsewhere. The cause of the sweat of blood lies elsewhere; the cup that he asked, if possible, to be spared from drinking lies elsewhere. The real bitterness of the cross is sin coming upon him along with what follows from sin: the Father's wrath and the Father's curse.

I have seen the Father gathering the iniquity of us all onto the Son (Isaiah 53:6), making him bear our sins in his body (1 Peter 2:24), making him, "for our sake, . . . to be sin" (2 Corinthians 5:21), weighing him down with our iniquities so that they mount up over his head and cause him to bend beneath the burden (see Psalm 38:4).

I have seen the Father, in order that he might redeem us from the curse of the law, making the Son to be a curse for us (Galatians 3:13), taking pleasure in crushing him (Isaiah 53:10), subjecting him to weariness, letting his hand weigh heavily on him, piercing him with his arrows; leaving no part of his flesh unharmed because of his indignation and no health in his bones because of sin (Psalm 38:2-3).

I have seen the Father from this point on finding in his Son—yes, in his only and beloved Son—a sight that repels his holy majesty. I have seen the Father distancing himself from the Son's deliverance and from his howling cries; leaving him to call out with his voice hoarse, his throat parched, his eyes dim with waiting (Psalm 69:3). Finally the Son is compelled to exclaim in agony: "*Eli, Eli, lema sabachthani?* . . . My God, my God, why have you forsaken me?" (Psalm 22:1, Matthew 27:46).

Does this too leave you with a dry eye and a cold heart? Then let me be given a different audience! Give me an audience of Greenlanders, of pagans, of Jews, hearing for the first time about the marvels of such a love, and you will see them moved, pierced by remorse, and crying out, "What must [we] do to be saved?" (Acts 16:30). Better still, give me the soil of the earth, give me the rocks, give me the curtain of the temple, give me the sun as listeners, and I will show you the earth shaking, the rocks splitting, the curtain being torn in two, and the sun hiding its face (Matthew 27:51,45). I will show you the universe—a witness to their mourning and to your indifference—asking itself if it wasn't for them rather than for you that the Son of God died!

Tell us, Greenlanders, pagans, Jews; tell us, earth, rocks, curtain of the temple, sun; the God who sent his Son as an atonement for our sins, what is this God if he is not love?

Love's Motive

But what finally manages to break Kajarnak's heart is the *reason* for this love. For in the end, if God has loved us that much, where does all this love come from? As for us, we love what is loveable, and above all we love those who love us. Were we loveable in God's eyes, or did we love him first? No. "This is love: not that we have loved God, but that he loved us" (1 John 4:10).

Nothing We Have Done

Kajarnak says to himself, "God sent his only Son into the world as a propitiation for my sins; and I, what have I done for him? What have I done to attract that love with which he meets me, satisfies me, overwhelms me? Where are my entitlements, my claims; where are my works, my desires, my thoughts that could provoke such a love on his part? When he remembered me, when he extended his favor toward me, when he sacrificed his own Son for me, when he sent me this missionary from across the seas to testify to me of his love; yesterday or even this morning, what was I doing? I was forgetting him, offending him, and trampling his holy law under foot. I was going astray, living in rebellion, in idolatry, in covetousness, in hatred, in lying, in stealing, in sensual pleasures. As to my claims, I see none but my sins; and as to my entitlements to his love, I see none but that love itself!"

Yes, Kajarnak, you're right, and the more you learn to know yourself, the more you will see yourself to be guilty, unrighteous, rebellious, "alienated and hostile in mind, doing evil deeds" (see Colossians 1:21), worthy in the end of hell and of an eternal curse. If you could have doubted it for a moment, the very sight of that cross before your eyes would suffice to disabuse you, for if it shows you God loving the sinner so much that he gave his only Son in order to save him, it also shows you God detesting sin so much that no lesser price than the death of his only Son could atone for it. The same blood measures both God's love for us and God's horror of our sins.

What awful sins they must be to subject God's Son to the rage of hell, to the fury of the world, and, alas, to the anger of heaven! What awful sins, if God could not look upon them in his own Son without crushing him—his very own Son—under the weight of his curse! The most dreadful declarations of God's hatred for sin—the world submerged by the flood, five cities of the plain consumed by fire from heaven, the entire population of Canaan exterminated, the thunder, lightening, smoke, and earthquake at Sinai—all that is small beside God's only Son dying on the cross.

Come close, Kajarnak, and learn to read in the agony of your Savior the nature of the hell that you deserved. And yet, when you were still so hateful that only the blood of the Son of God could reconcile you with God, God loved you so much that he shed that precious blood for you! "Is this the manner of man?" (2 Samuel 7:19 KJV). You have been able to love a wife, a child, a friend. But to love an enemy, to pursue him with your love until you have triumphed over his hatred;

to sacrifice your most precious treasure for him when his animosity for you is at its strongest? Have you ever done, have you ever seen, have you ever imagined anything like that? God loved you, not for something loveable that he saw in you, but in spite of all that he saw that was evil and detestable. He loved you because of himself, by an outpouring of his nature. He loved you because he is love.

Pure Grace!

Kajarnak is not the only one to be moved by this thought. All the sacred writers share a single voice on this; and in the tender descriptions that they give of God's love, the significant point, the thing that pierces their own hearts, is how free and unmerited that love is.

"We all once . . . were by nature children of wrath, like the rest of mankind. But God, being rich in mercy, because of the great love with which he loved us, even when we were dead in our trespasses, made us alive together with Christ—by grace you have been saved" (Ephesians 2:3-5).

And elsewhere: "For while we were still weak, at the right time Christ died for the ungodly. For one will scarcely die for a righteous person—though perhaps for a good person one would dare even to die—but God shows his love for us in that while we were still sinners, Christ died for us" (Romans 5:6-8).

And yet again: "For we ourselves were once foolish, disobedient, led astray, slaves to various passions and pleasures, passing our days in malice and envy, hated by others and hating one another. But when the goodness and loving kindness of God our Savior appeared, he saved us, not because of works done by us in righteousness, but according to his own mercy." (Titus 3:3-5).

But all of that yields to the expression of our apostle: "In this is love, not that we have loved God but that he loved us" (1 John 4:10). Do you feel the force of the thought, "In this is love"? What we have seen up to now—a propitiation found for our sins, God's Son sent into the world, the Son delivered up for our sins—all that is a manifestation of God's love; a manifestation so striking that all other marks of divine love that a man or even an angel could gather together from the entire universe pale beside it. But here is something more than a manifestation of love. Here is its very essence and nature: God "first loved us" (1 John 4:19). If the grandeur of that love forces us to cry out with admiration, "God so loved the world, that he gave his only Son" (John 3:16), the freeness of that same love drags from our humiliated and broken hearts that tender and profound statement, "God is love!"

God Is Love!

Yes, God is love. That alone can explain how much he has loved . . . who? The angels? The saints? No, but us, his enemies; we ourselves; I who speak to you and you who listen.

God is love. Love is his being, his substance, his life.

God is love. Love sums up all his works and explains all his ways. Love inspired the creation of a holy race and the redemption of a fallen race. Love conquered nothingness in order to give us existence and triumphed over sin in order to give us eternal life. Love is the subject of the angels' admiration, and love will be the subject of ours in eternity. God's thoughts are love, his will is love, his providence is love, his dispensations are love, his holiness is love, his judgments are love. Everything in him is love. "God is love" (1 John 4:8,16).

Savoring God's Love

But Kajarnak's heart tells him more than all of our discourses. Here is this pagan—if we can still call him by this name—hearing the good news and hanging on the missionary's words. With his heart moved and his conscience troubled, he cries out, "What did you say? Repeat that for us. I, too, want to be saved!" Why him and not you? Why should this same doctrine that turned a pagan into a Christian on the coast of Greenland not turn more than one nominal Christian today in France, in this assembly, into an alive, spiritual Christian?

OUR PRIVILEGED POSITION

In order to awaken you from your normal apathy, I have invited you to put yourselves in the place of this Greenlander who is hearing the gospel for the first time in his life. But beware of thinking that such a condition is indispensable for being touched by the gospel or that the gospel has lost its power from having been proclaimed to you so often. Beware of thinking that this coldness that we were deploring in you a while ago is a necessary part of your position. It is a necessary part of sin, of carelessness, of ingratitude, of unbelief, and of nothing more.

Your position is a privilege, if you only knew how to respond to it, and you can as soon as you want to. Have you often heard the gospel repeated to you? Well then, you have just what Kajarnak so ardently desired: "Repeat that for us, repeat that for us." Make up for the lack of novelty by the fervor of your meditations, and you will discover that in your long experience with the gospel you have a means of being all the more permeated with God's love.

Men's works lose something when examined too closely; but no matter how closely you admire God's works, the testimonies of his love and, above all, the unspeakable gift of his Son, you will always remain well below the truth. There are so many new facets to contemplate that all the sermons, all the books, all the meditations would not suffice to exhaust them any more than you could empty the sea using the hollow of your hand!

The Riches of God's Love

Sometimes it is the depth of the abyss from which God has drawn us. What amazing love, to have delivered us from sin, from hell, from the eternal fire, from the company of the devil and his angels! "Great is your steadfast love toward me; you have delivered my soul from the depths of Sheol" (Psalm 86:13)!

Sometimes it is the number, the enormity of the gifts that go along with that of the Son. What amazing love, to grant us "grace upon grace" (John 1:16), eternal life, peace, light, strength, joy, and, to sum it up in a word, "participation in the divine nature" (see 2 Peter 1:4)!

Sometimes it is the grandeur, the fullness of the pardon that God gives us in Jesus Christ. What amazing love, to annihilate sin, to "cast all our sins into the depths of the sea" (Micah 7:19), to remove them from us "as far as the east is from the west" (Psalm 103:12), to ask only that we repent and believe. When we have fallen to our knees beneath the weight of the divine curse, it raises us up freed, justified, glorified, and saved!

Sometimes it is the new direction that God's grace in Jesus Christ imparts to those anguishes of life that we inherit from the first Adam. What amazing love, to lay hold of all those fruits of sin, to cause them to serve his plan, to force them to increase our joy, to turn the curse into a blessing. It constrains all creatures, even our greatest enemies, to work now only for our good (see Romans 8:28)!

Sometimes it is the individual calls that God addresses to each of us, leading us to receive this great salvation. What amazing love—seeing that we are slow to flee the coming wrath—to send us call after call, warning after warning, messenger after messenger, affliction after affliction, if need be, and to knock time after time at the door of our hearts!

Sometimes it is the firm assurance of grace that the Holy Spirit communicates to a soul, even to the soul of a Zacchaeus, a Mary Magdalene, or a crucified robber. What amazing love, to enable such a soul to lay hold of eternal life, to be resurrected ahead of time,[5] to take possession of paradise, to be seated in the heavenly places with Jesus Christ! What amazing love, to enable a soul to sing, "I am sure that neither death nor life, nor angels nor rulers, nor things present nor things to come, nor powers, nor height nor depth, nor anything else in all creation, will be able to separate us from the love of God in Christ Jesus our Lord" (Romans 8:38-39).

LOVE'S GREATEST TREASURE

But above all, above all, what amazing love, to have given, to have sacrificed for us the only and beloved Son! This is where we must always return. This is where every grace and the fullness of heaven are focused, for "he who did not spare his own Son but gave him up for us all, how will he not also with him graciously give us all things?" (Romans 8:32).

This is where, "in the face of Jesus Christ" (2 Corinthians 4:6) and of Jesus Christ crucified, we behold with unveiled face the love hidden within the bosom of the Father. This is where the heart of God is opened before us and we read there, as in a book, unspeakable things that no human language can adequately express. This is where we receive a new scale for measuring the love for which all of the combined human measures are inadequate, and where, "being rooted and grounded in love, [we] may have strength to comprehend with all the saints what is the breadth and length and height and depth, and to know the love of Christ that surpasses knowledge" (Ephesians 3:17-19).

And yet, what a futile effort! No, we could never behold him without a veil! Our weak hearts couldn't endure it! No

---

[5] As Monod expounds at length in the next chapter, he regards the resurrection not as an historical event in the life of a believer, but as a new inner and permanent life. It is Jesus' own life within us.

mortal man could see such love and live! Our entire being would be broken and annihilated by it! Down here we gaze only on its borders! And if, like Moses, we ask God to let us see his glory, he will cause all his goodness to pass before our eyes, but we will not be able to see it directly. While such a sight is being spread out before us, God will put us in a cleft in the rock and cover us with his hand (see Exodus 33:22). Yet a voice will strike our ears; no longer the voice that Moses heard, but a sweeter, more tender voice, the voice of the Holy Spirit in our text saying, "God is love! God is love!"

Responding to God's Love

And now, what do you want to do with such love? Do you want to respond to it as Kajarnak did and say, "I, too, want to be saved"?

Believe Because It Is Unbelievable

I'm not asking whether you believe in the truth of the doctrine that the Lord has just caused you to hear. That doctrine bears too clear a witness to itself for you to have any doubts about it. If it were not true, it would not be in the world, for these are things that "no eye has seen, nor ear heard, nor the heart of man imagined" (1 Corinthians 2:9). Man's having thought up such a plan would be more inexplicable than God's having carried it out.

Even in saying this, I realize that the very greatness of the love that God has shown us in the gospel makes the gospel unbelievable for many. God giving his only Son, this Son taking on our nature, this Son dying for our sins—that is too much love, too infinite a condescension to find full acceptance in hearts like ours that are enslaved to self.

How can we believe that God loved us first, if we love only those who love us? How can we believe that God has removed our sins, if we tenaciously harbor the memory of offenses against us? How can we believe that God gave his only and beloved Son for us, if we are so slow to give to others, let me not say an only and beloved son, but a little of our time, our labor, our necessities, our excess, our well-being?

Yes, but think about it and you will recognize that the very things that stir up our unbelief are those that should confound it. For, in the end, how could the human spirit have imagined such a marvel of love that surpasses and overflows it on all sides? How would the human spirit be capable of inventing that which it is not even able to believe? Where would it have gotten this shocking idea of a Son of God placed on a cross for our sins?—in what unknown territory, in what convolution of its meditations, in what depths of its philosophies, in what dream of its poets?

Ah, though I should find this plan of the gospel in the middle of a desert, far from the prophets who proclaimed it, far from the wonders that attest to it, I would immediately recognize it as the work of a God whose ways are not our ways and whose thoughts are not our thoughts. When God loves, he loves as he does everything else, as God. Does he want to display his power? He divides the waters of the sea. Does he want to make his justice shine forth? He causes a flood to rise over the entire earth. Does he want to unfurl his glory? He speaks, and a world emerges out of nothing. Does he want to demonstrate that he is sovereign master? He speaks again, and the sun is extinguished and "the skies roll up like a scroll" (Isaiah 34:4). And does he want to manifest his love, which is "above all these" things (Colossians 3:14)? He sends his Son into the world and delivers him up for our sins.

Set Your Heart Free

Therefore, lay aside all your doubts, all your sophisms, all your hesitations. Do what Kajarnak did: listen to your heart, and you will be faithful. Do you not sense that your heart is bound up within you? It lacks air, daylight, and life. Set it free! Exchange the cold God, the dead God that you have served until now for the God who is love and who has given his Son in order to save you.

Come to the one who first "came to seek and to save the lost" (Luke 19:10), to the one who gives you this tender invitation: "Come, everyone who thirsts, come to the waters; and he who has no money, come, buy and eat! Come, buy wine and milk without money and without price" (Isaiah 55:1). Come, "and it will be given to you. Good measure, pressed down, shaken together, running over, will be put into your lap" (Luke 6:38). Come, such as you are; it is enough that you have heard the gospel for the first time. Kajarnak had heard it no more than that. All that is asked of you is to say as he did, "I, too, want to be saved." All that is asked is that you believe in God's love, that you enter into the plan of his grace, and that you do not make "the blood of his cross" (Colossians 1:20) useless. Today, here, in this place, believe, open yourself, abandon yourself, surrender yourself!

Do Not Presume Upon God's Love

And if you will not surrender, what then is your thinking? Could it be—please allow me to pose a question that presents itself to my spirit and that faithfulness prevents me from holding back—could it be that you are basing a secret calculation on that very love? Could it be that you encourage yourself in your unbelief by the thought that a God so full of love would be unable to reserve a miserable eternity for you? If that is the case, we will not refrain from explaining how unworthy this calculation is.

Be careful not to compare God to those weak persons whose ill-considered goodness indulges and nourishes the vice or the ingratitude that abuses it. That goodness is unworthy of a righteous man and more unworthy of a magistrate of integrity. How much more again is it unworthy of "the Judge of all the earth" (Genesis 18:25)?

God's love is a holy love which is united with a horror of sin, and nowhere—again, neither in the flood, nor in Sodom and Gomorrah, nor in Egypt, nor in Canaan, nor in Sinai— has that horror been so openly proclaimed as on the cross. If you remain in your sins and unbelief, God's love will find no way to reach you, and God cannot give you grace. He cannot do it without veiling his holiness and failing to be himself. He cannot do it, just as Jesus "could do no mighty work" among the Nazarenes "because of their unbelief" (Mark 6:5,6).[6] He cannot do it because you will have "rejected the purpose of God for [your]selves" (Luke 7:30). It is written, "If we are faithless, he remains faithful—for he cannot deny himself" (2 Timothy 2:13).

God's Love Transforms Us

But "though we speak in this way, yet in your case, beloved, we feel sure of better things—things that belong to salvation" (Hebrews 6:9). Isn't it true that you no longer want to close your heart to God's love or to live without faith before a God who is love? By such faith you will save your soul, and by it you will also become a different person. As you look upon God's love, it will communicate itself to you and will renew your entire being. It is in sensing oneself to be loved that one learns to love. Self-centeredness reigns only because we are ignorant of God's love: "Anyone who does not love does not know God" (1 John 4:8). You will love as you have been loved. You will love God, because God has first loved you. You will love your neighbor, because God has loved you both. Do you glimpse the new life that this change opens up for you?

---

[6] See also Matthew 13:58. [A.M.]

IMITATORS OF CHRIST

I see you as "imitators of God, as beloved children" (Ephesians 5:1), no longer living for anything except to pour out around you the love with which God has filled your hearts. I see you, following the example of Christ who loved you, "going about doing good" (see Acts 10:38) and finding your joy in privation, in fatigue, and in the sacrifices of charity. I see you "controlled by the love of Christ" (see 2 Corinthians 5:14); weaned from your self-will, from the love of money, and from the empty pleasures of the world; consoling the afflicted, relieving the poor, visiting the sick, and carrying Jesus Christ and all his blessings with you wherever you go.

Then the image and resemblance of God will have been formed anew in your heart! Then you will dwell in God and God in you! If being loved is the life of our soul, to love is its joy. If being loved is all the doctrine of the gospel, then to love is all of its ethic. To love as we have been loved is heaven on earth until such time as it becomes heaven in heaven.

DEEP JOY

Happy are you if God's love penetrates you so fully that one can find no better definition of your character—from whatever angle he looks at you—than the one that love inspired Saint John to use in describing God's character! Happy are you if someone can say of you, "He is love! His words are love! His works are love! His zeal is love! His labor is love! His joys are love! His tears are love! His reproaches are love! His judgments are love!" Happy are you, above all, if God "who searches mind and heart" (Revelation 2:23) can add, "His heart is love, too!" Amen.

I am the Resurrection and the Life[1]

※

(Paris, Easter, 1855)

John 11:25-26

Jesus said to her, "I am the resurrection and the life. Whoever believes in me, though he die, yet shall he live, and everyone who lives and believes in me shall never die. Do you believe this?"

Breaking the Reign of Death

A World Where Death Reigns

We live in a world where death reigns. It is a small matter that death's presence overturns all our plans and brings an end for us to everything on earth. Even in its absence, it saddens everything. That inevitable end never disappears from before our eyes.

---

[1] Monod preached this Easter sermon just a year before his death from cancer at age 54. From this point on, he seems to have preached only one other public sermon, on Pentecost, seven weeks after Easter, and only portions of that sermon have survived.

A child has just been given to us, but he is born to die. A healing has just been granted to us, but it will last only until death. A friendship is our consolation, but it must be broken, perhaps any day now, by death. And since all that we do ends in death, one could say that we live only to die.

If the joys of life bear the mark of death, what of its pains? There is not one of them that does not turn our eyes toward death, for they will all rush into its bosom like brooks flowing into a common river. Where does that sickness lead? To death. Where does that dejection of body and spirit lead? To death. That fatigue, those privations, that hunger, that thirst? To death. Those years of toil, that weakening of the senses, that trembling of the hands? To death.

That dreadful name is written on everything that happens to us. It is even written on our very persons. Whoever learns to read our lines and wrinkles will find inscribed on each and every forehead, like the demolition notice on a condemned building, "Death." All the world's diversions—its shows, its novels, its holidays—are designed to distract us from this fact, but we might just as well relate to ourselves in order to take our minds off ourselves. It never works, and the efforts to which one is reduced in order not to see death only serve to underscore how impossible it is to remove it from view. Humanity depicted in its natural state is condemned to lifelong slavery through fear of death (see Hebrews 2:15).

A Man Who Removes Death

But out of the midst of this fallen and dying race, behold, a man arises who boasts of nothing less than removing death for whoever agrees to commit himself to him alone. Either that is the raving of a sick mind or else it is the most marvelous deliverance of which mankind has ever heard. The first hypothesis is possible for those who have never opened Holy Scripture, while only the second remains for those who have listened to the Son of man and glimpsed in him the Holy of holies.[2] Moreover, consider his words: "I am the resurrection and the life. Whoever believes in me, though he die, yet shall he live, and everyone who lives and believes in me shall never die." This is not the language of presumptuous confidence. It is the language of firm but peaceful assurance.

In the face of such solemn, such penetrating words, I feel free only to follow them step by step. I will be fortunate if I am allowed to understand them and to enable you to understand them, without in any way straying from the Master's thoughts!

I find three things here: a principle set forth, "I am the resurrection and the life;" the application of that principle to believers such as Lazarus, who have died, "Whoever believes in me, though he die, yet shall he live;" and the application to believers like Martha, who are still alive, "everyone who lives and believes in me shall never die." Let us consider each of these in turn.

Resurrection Life

To really understand the words, "I am the resurrection and the life," we need to put them back into the context that gave rise to them.

More Than a Return to Earthly Life

Martha is filled with regret that Jesus had not been forewarned about Lazarus' death so that he could heal him of

---

[2] This seems to be an allusion to the innermost part of the Old Testament tabernacle, the place where God's glory resided on earth as it later did in Jesus' person during his incarnation.

his illness. Thus she has no sooner met him (for in her impatience she had gone out to meet him), than she says to him, "Lord, if you had been here, my brother would not have died" (John 11:21).[3]

But mingled with Martha's regret is a vague hope that he who could have healed her brother can also return him to life as he had did the widow of Nain's son (Luke 7:14) and as he did Jairus' daughter (Matthew 9:25). The pain of having lost Lazarus from earth and the desire to recover him on earth are alone what fill Martha's soul. Here we recognize Martha as Saint Luke paints her (Luke 10:38-40), sincerely attached to Jesus Christ but still only slightly detached from this life.

Jesus intentionally gives her an answer less precise than the one she wanted: "Your brother will rise again" (John 11:23). This could apply to a future life as well as to this present life. Martha is insistent, and the passing but present deliverance that completely preoccupies her causes her to treat the eternal but future deliverance as a second order blessing. It cannot satisfy her. "I know that he will rise again in the resurrection on the last day" (John 11:24).

This is when Jesus, wishing to turn Martha's gaze from her brother onto her Savior, speaks that profound word destined to make her seek in Jesus himself the basis of her hopes for a resurrection. Previously those hopes were wandering off after the creature and after the life of this world, but now he says to her, "I am the resurrection and the life" (John 11:25).

---

[3] This expression of regret perhaps includes an indirect and timid reproach. Jesus, warned by Martha and Mary about their brother's illness, had delayed going to answer their appeal. He did so specifically to have the opportunity to conquer death on this occasion, rather than to prevent it (see John 11:15). [A.M.]

An Inner and Permanent Life

With these words, Jesus throws a completely new light into Martha's soul as to the nature of the resurrection. It is not a fact of our outward existence but the principle of an inner and permanent life; a life that resides in Jesus and communicates itself from Jesus to the one who believes in him.

Completely absorbed in her brother, Martha can only seek the moment when he will be awakened from the dead and given back to her. The only question for her is whether she has already reached that desired moment or whether she must wait for it on the other side of the tomb. This logic would reduce the resurrection to the beggarly proportions of an historical event. On the one hand, the resurrection at the last day is an event for which one must wait a long time, while on the other hand, the immediate resurrection to which Martha shows herself to be all too attached is an event that will last only a few days.

Neither a resurrection that we must wait for until after death nor a resurrection that we tremble each day to lose through death is the true resurrection. We do not wait for the true resurrection, because it has already arrived for the believer. Nor is it lost, because it resides in the inexhaustible depths of his being. It is not an historical event; it is a spiritual condition and a fruit of faith.

Here, the life that Jesus links to the resurrection is what elsewhere he sometimes calls "eternal life" and sometimes simply "life." When that life is confronted by death and triumphs over it, it takes on the name of resurrection. Thus the resurrection and the life in my text are not two different things but one and the same thing—life—considered in two different aspects; sometimes on its own, continuing without hindrance, and sometimes as surmounting the interruption that death claims to bring to its course. "I am the resurrection, because I am the life."

Jesus, Its Source and Essence

As Jesus is enlightening Martha regarding the nature of the true resurrection, he so closely associates that resurrection and life to his own person that no one can seek them except in him. Whether she seeks a resurrection for Lazarus or for herself, it is neither to Lazarus nor to herself that Martha must look. It is to Jesus Christ alone.

But there is more, and the connection is even closer than I have made it out to be. Jesus Christ does not say, "I am the giver of life," or "I am the author of the resurrection." He says, "I am the resurrection and the life," just as elsewhere he says, "I am the light" (John 8:12, 9:5); "I am the truth; I am the life" (see John 14:6). These sovereign and infinite goods to which the human soul instinctively aspires are dim memories of a better state from which it has fallen. Light, truth, life, holiness, love—Jesus is their very essence because he is the essence of divinity, the one in whom "the whole fullness of deity dwells bodily" (Colossians 2:9).

Jesus seems to be saying to Martha, "Don't go seeking elsewhere for that resurrection you so much desire, whether for your brother or for yourself. Don't ask it of the present, or of the future, or of this world, or of the next. Gaze only on me; I am right here with you, yet you don't seem to have known me up to now. It is all in me. It *is* me and I am it. Whoever possesses me, possesses the resurrection. 'Whoever has the Son has life' (1 John 5:12). Did your brother have me when he was dying? Then be at peace about him; he has life even though he is dead. Do you possess me yourself, you who are living? Then don't be afraid; you cannot die, even in dying."

Let us not try to probe any further. There are things that are sensed better than they are defined. But let us imagine the impression of solemnity, respect, and confidence that must have seized Martha's soul in hearing her Master say, "I am the one who is the resurrection and the life. Whoever believes in me, though he die, yet shall he live, and everyone who lives and believes in me shall never die. Do you believe this?" (John 11:26). Thus she responds with the simple expression of her faith in him, "I believe that you are the Christ, the Son of God, who is coming into the world" (John 11:27), and she stops questioning him.

Received Through Faith

Jesus' last question, along with Martha's response, gives a clear understanding of how we can share this power of resurrection and life that exists in Jesus. It is by faith. The one who believes has life because he possesses Jesus; the one who does not believe does not have life because he does not possess him.

Just as this language elevates Jesus above the common perceptions that one has of him and of his word, so too it elevates true faith above the ordinary notions attached to it. If Jesus only brought to earth a truer doctrine and a purer morality than those that were known before he came, then faith might well be only the belief in the one and the acceptance of the other. But if Jesus is the living reality of that which is in God, if he is "the truth, the light, the resurrection, the life," then it follows necessarily that faith is a personal appropriation of Jesus Christ and of all that is in him.

In himself, Jesus is the resurrection and the life; but for the one who doesn't believe, this treasure might as well not exist, because he doesn't come to Jesus Christ and doesn't enter into relationship with him. On the other hand, the one who believes comes to him, unites himself to him, and becomes one with him just as he is one with the Father. He receives Jesus, nourishes himself on him, and gains a share in his life: "Because I live, you also will live" (John 14:19). How could we be astonished at the grandeur of the promises made to a faith that is so great and so new? And yet that all-powerful faith is none other than the completely simple faith of the least in the kingdom of God: "I believe that you are the Christ, the Son of God, who is coming into the world." It is so powerful because it is so simple.

JESUS' EASTER AND OURS

Don't think that I am straying from today's holiday.[4] The declaration on which we are meditating is directly related to it and sheds new light on it. We are accustomed to saying that the Father raises the Son from the dead by the power of the Holy Spirit in order to demonstrate who the Son is and to reassure us of the efficacy of his sacrifice. That's true, but it doesn't exhaust the matter. The Easter event occurs because Jesus *is* the resurrection and the life.

Jesus is not resurrected as the Shunamite woman's son or as the young man from Nain or as Lazarus himself were, in obedience to an external voice, though it be the voice of God himself. Jesus' resurrection has its explanation within him. It is in the very necessity of things. Because he is the Prince of Life, it is contradictory that he should be held by the bonds of death. That is why he says, "No one takes it from me, but I lay it down of my own accord. I have authority to lay it down, and I have authority to take it up again" (John 10:18).

Will I dare to say that this relates also to you in your own way and that God has an Easter in store for you too, whoever you are who believe in Jesus Christ? We have just seen that through such faith Jesus himself dwells within you. Henceforth, things are the same for you as they are for Jesus; or rather they are the same for Jesus as they are for Jesus: "Jesus Christ is the same yesterday and today and forever" (Hebrews 13:8). Whether he is within you or outside of you

---

[4] This sermon was given on Easter Sunday in 1855, just a year before Monod's death.

or wherever he might be, he is the life, and in the presence of death he is the resurrection.

For you who believe in him, that life is in you and cannot cease. It is a life to which the life of this world can add nothing and from which the death of this world can take nothing. If you are laid in the tomb, you must be raised from it again, not simply as Lazarus was, because the voice of Jesus will call to you, "Lazarus, come out" (John 11:43), but rather as Jesus himself was. You must be raised by the necessity inherent in your being, by the presence in you of him who could not be held by the bonds of death. Oh, grace! Oh, mystery! I have tried hard to bring light to it, but I cannot. Yet that which I cannot express, do you not sense it?

The Believer Sheltered from Death

Jesus never loses himself in theories. Even in these sublime perspectives whose heights leave the highest maxims of human philosophy well below them, he always has the instruction, the consolation, and the sanctification of those who belong to him in view. He would not disdain to open heaven and gather all of its light in order to illumine the smallest step or dissipate the tiniest cloud from the least of his disciples. Having thus posed the heavenly principle, "I am the resurrection and the life," Jesus hastens to make the practical application for Martha, to reassure her first with regard to Lazarus and then, secondarily, with regard to herself. For Lazarus: the believer who is dead still lives. For Martha: the believer who is living will never die.[5]

At their heart, these two applications are only one. To say that Lazarus, who is dead, has not ceased to live or that

---

[5] This is how one must translate the last words of my text, and the timid translation of one of our versions, "will surely not die forever," was dictated by fear of such an astonishing doctrine, in spite of grammar and healthy interpretation. [A.M.]

Martha, who lives, will not die is to proclaim the same principle. The only difference is one of time and situation. The principle is that the life of Jesus within the believer is sheltered from the assaults of death. But since Jesus makes a distinction between these two aspects of the same truth, let us distinguish them as well, in order to learn from him to console ourselves both for those with faith in Christ who have left us and for ourselves who are still living in that same faith.

LAZARUS: LIFE EVEN IN DEATH

"Whoever believes, though he die, yet shall he live," and Lazarus, though dead, lives. When Jesus says with regard to Jairus' daughter, "She is not dead but sleeping" (Luke 8:52), he seems to be indicating nothing more than his intention to raise her up, so that in his sovereign authority he changes death into sleep. But this same statement with regard to Lazarus, "Our friend Lazarus has fallen asleep, but I go to awaken him" (John 11:11), hides a deeper meaning that Jesus unveils in talking to Martha: this sleep of death is suitable for the believer. Saint Paul will speak in the same way later on (1 Corinthians 11:30, marginal reading; 1 Thessalonians 4:13-14). Lazarus is dead only according to men, who do not see the true principle of life. To God, who sees that principle, he is merely asleep.

LIFE THAT SLEEPS

A man who sleeps offers certain signs by which we distinguish him from a corpse and which guarantee to us that his senses, though momentarily chained in immobility, will gently and effortlessly shake it off after nature has taken the necessary rest. In the same way, God recognizes in Lazarus—dead, immobile, and whose corpse is already decomposing—a principle of life that faith in Jesus has placed within him.

This principle distinguishes him from another dead person lying beside him; one into whom Jesus has not been summoned by faith.

It is not that the second dead person lacks a principle of existence that will come alive again at Jesus' voice, but that existence is not "the life." The external Jesus that will call to him will not find in him a corresponding internal Jesus. Thus he will hear Jesus' voice and will leave his tomb, but he will leave it for "the resurrection of judgment," not for "the resurrection of life" (John 5:29). Lazarus will leave in a totally different way. He is only asleep. He will awaken for a resurrection of life, and this awakening will come in God's time, when the sleep has had time to accomplish its restorative work.

For the sleep of death is not lost. It shelters God's elect from the tempter just as snow protects the fruit of the earth from the cold of winter. Though he doesn't in any way stir, though all that you see of him has fallen into dissolution, the life of Jesus is in him. You would see it, if your eyes were not confined to this earthly existence by the bonds of the flesh. The reason that you are excluded from all communication with him is not so much in his state as in your weakness. It is not that he lacks life; it is that you, in your present condition, lack the ability to discern it. It is almost like a man who, through weakness of his senses or lack of intelligence, would be incapable of discriminating a sleeping man from a dead one.

Already Victors

Whatever the case, Lazarus lives. While waiting to be awakened, he is already completely victorious over death, completely freed from condemnation, and no longer having to appear before God's tribunal except to be assigned his place of bliss. "Truly, truly, I say to you, whoever hears my word and believes him who sent me has eternal life. He does not come into judgment, but has passed from death to life" (John 5:24). This is the consolation that Jesus offers to Martha in the death of Lazarus. How much more precious this consolation is than the added one he is going to give her; the one of seeing him interrupt his sleep this very hour and leave the tomb. The benefit of the miracle is worth less than that of grace. The added consolation will be short, like earthly life, since sooner or later she must either lose Lazarus again or be lost to him—to speak after the manner of men. On the other hand, from the point of view of the resurrection and the life which are in Jesus, "he was parted from them for a while, that she might have him back forever" (see Philemon 15).

Moreover, if Jesus grants Martha this momentary consolation while teaching her not to value it too highly, it is in order to demonstrate in the person of Lazarus the very doctrine we just set forth. You doubt that the death of the believer is only sleep? Very well! In order to convince your unbelief, here is someone whom I am going to awaken. It would have been better for him to continue in the sweet sleep that he was tasting in my bosom, but it is worth more to you that he awakens so that you might be instructed. Now you can know by this single example, without troubling the sleep of the many other saints who are sleeping in me, how tranquil you can be about them.

Yes, my brothers, that is a true consolation with regard to our dead who have died in Jesus (for Jesus is only speaking of such). "But we do not want you to be uninformed, brothers, about those who are asleep, that you may not grieve as others do who have no hope. For since we believe that Jesus died and rose again, even so, through Jesus, God will bring with him those who have fallen asleep" (1 Thessalonians 4:13-14). He does not even want their sleep to give the slightest advantage to the saints who are still living when Jesus Christ appears. "We who are alive, who are left until the coming of the Lord" (that is how the apostle designates the generation alive at the second coming of Jesus Christ; whatever generation it might be, it is his through brotherly love) "will not precede those who have fallen asleep. For the Lord himself will descend from heaven. . . . And the dead in Christ will rise first. Then we who are alive . . . will be caught up together with them . . . to meet the Lord . . . and so we will always be with the Lord. Therefore encourage one another with these words" (1 Thessalonians 4:15-18).

Alive!

Yes, encourage one another, and may you not regard "the comforts of God [as] too small for you" (Job 15:11). He who has believed in Jesus, though he is dead, yet he lives. Your Lazarus isn't dead; he lives. Those old people, those fathers and mothers in Israel who have gone to sleep in Jesus "full of days" (1 Chronicles 23:1, etc.)—they are not dead; they live. Those servants of Jesus Christ who were gathered up in their prime and in the midst of their work—they are not dead; they live. Those young men, those young women who said goodbye to you while placing their weary heads on Jesus breast—they are not dead; they live. Those small children who have gone on before you, babbling the name of Jesus with their childish voices—they are not dead; they live.

All those saints, all those martyrs, all those faithful ones whom the Lord has called to himself in past generations—they are not dead; they live. Those bountiful confessors of Jesus Christ whose blood has been poured out like water on the unhappy soil of our France by an idolatrous and fallen church—they are not dead; they live. Luther, Calvin, Wycliffe, Huss, Jerome of Prague, and all those witnesses of obscure ages—they are not dead; they live. Saint Bernard, Saint Ambrose, Saint Augustine, Saint Chrysostom, Saint Athanasius, and all those great lights of the first centuries—

they are not dead; they live. Paul, Peter, John, James, Timothy, and all the apostles—they are not dead; they live.

Beyond that, all the prophets, all the believers of the Old Testament, hoping in this Christ who was to come—they are not dead, they live. Isaiah lives, Ezekiel lives, Daniel lives, Jacob lives, Abraham lives, Noah lives, Abel lives. They don't live according to the flesh, but they live according to the Spirit. They don't live for men, but they live for the Lord. They don't live with regard to appearances, but they live with regard to reality.

Picture in your minds the invisible world, the only true and permanent world, populated, filled up with all these dead who live. Find, if you can, a society in which it is more desirable for you to gain entry than this one; and while waiting to enter it, don't weep over those who are there; they live. Weep for yourselves and for your children who are here, dragging around a life that is always dying. Weep tears of holy impatience to go and join not only those men of God "of whom the world was not worthy" (Hebrews 11:38), but the One who is their resurrection, their life, and their common bliss!

Martha: The Living Sheltered From Death

Jesus could have stopped with the application he had just made of the great truth of our text to Lazarus' condition. Martha's preoccupation went no further than her brother, and that was enough to address it, at least to the extent he considered it appropriate to do so. But, like God and like the disciples who are animated by his love, Jesus is in the habit of giving more than was asked of him. Jesus is asked if it is necessary to pay tribute to Caesar. He answers, "Render to Caesar the things that are Caesar's," and he adds, "and to God the things that are God's" (Matthew 22:21). The jailer asks Saint Paul what he must do to be saved. Saint Paul answers, "Believe in the Lord Jesus, and you will be saved," and he adds, "you and your household" (Acts 16:31). Martha wants to be reassured about Lazarus, and Jesus, having satisfied this need (if she could hear him), adds something to reassure her about herself: "Everyone who lives and believes in me shall never die."

Never to Die

Who but Jesus, with his divine assurance in the divine truth of his word, would dare to say to one of his disciples beaten down by bitter mourning, "You believe in me, therefore have peace. You will never die"? Once again, is this some fanatic, some insane person—or is he the Prince of life, the living and true God? Make your choice. You spirits who are perhaps still wavering, still hindered, scattered throughout this Christian audience, I ask you again, "Does this choice still seem doubtful to you?" Such assurance coupled with such profound humility, with such true renouncement, with superhuman love, with divine holiness; does it not bear witness to itself? And if you persist in total unbelief or in a full refusal to investigate these things, do you not pronounce in advance over yourselves Jesus' judgment: "Whoever does not believe is condemned already, because he has not believed in the name of the only Son of God. And this is the judgment: the light has come into the world, and people loved the darkness rather than the light because their deeds were evil" (John 3:18-19)?

Whatever the case, Martha has the weakness and the simplicity to believe that the truth is true, that holiness is holy, that life is alive, and that God is God. That is what opens her heart, and what will open the heart of every believer who hears me, to that astonishing and magnificent promise: "Everyone who lives and believes in me shall never die."

He will, no doubt, die with regard to the flesh, with regard to men, with regard to appearances, just as Lazarus did. But with regard to the spirit, with regard to God, with regard to reality, he will not die any more than Lazarus is dead. He cannot die, because he bears within him a life over which the external world has no hold. That life is Jesus whom he possesses and on whom he is nourished by faith.

Why am I making distinctions that Jesus doesn't judge it appropriate to make? Does he need me to make excuses for his language or to justify its boldness? Surely not. If he keeps silent about the question of the flesh, of men, and of appearances, it is because he has not come into the world to be concerned with the earthly and transitory side of things. He borrows its language, but he doesn't borrow its thoughts. The words of human language are like vessels that earth provides for him, but he fills them with the truths of heaven. Don't be astonished, then, that he himself takes account only of the eternal and pure essence of things. This is all that he came for; this is the only environment in which he moves. He who "ascended into heaven" (John 3:13) speaks from heaven, unlike his inspired instruments, who are "of the earth . . . and [speak] in an earthly way" (John 3:31). Therefore let us leave Jesus all the power of his language in order to leave Martha all the fullness of her consolation. She believes, she will never die; and we who believe, we will never die.

JESUS' GATEWAY TO A NEW LIFE

In order to grasp this lovely doctrine better, let us try to transport ourselves to the place where Jesus approaches his cross and into his inner man. He walks toward death, toward the most awful death that can be conceived, toward a death whose physical suffering can only be surpassed by its mental anguish. He walks toward a death that, nonetheless, was foreseen, even to its smallest detail, and thus was present even before it arrived. And, finally, he walks toward a death that is so terrible for both his human and divine natures that, in seeing it face to face, he at first shrinks back from it, crying out, "If it be possible, let this cup pass from me" (Matthew 26:39), while sweat mingled with blood flows from his whole body.

What is it that sustains him in his agony? Above all, it is the awareness of accomplishing the Father's will, but this awareness does not exclude for him and ought not to exclude for his disciple the encouragements found in his personal circumstances. That same divine foresight that makes Jesus contemplate ahead of time all the bitterness of his cross causes him equally to contemplate, beyond the cross and even through the cross, the glory of the resurrection and of all that must follow it—his ascension, his Church, the pouring out of his Spirit, the founding of his Kingdom, his final triumph. This vision of resurrection and life, except during the brief battles of Gethsemane and Golgotha—no, even in their very midst—softens and sweetens the horror of the cross, dominating and absorbing it.

Is it for Jesus a question of himself? "For the joy set before him, [he] endured the cross, despising the shame," and for that price he "is seated at the right hand of the throne of God" (Hebrews 12:2). Is it for him a question of his Church? He finds his peace in considering that this cross is the only path through which he can bring eternal life into a world enslaved by death. "Truly, truly, I say to you, unless a grain of wheat falls into the earth and dies, it remains alone; but if it dies, it bears much fruit" (John 12:24).

The sight of his imminent death is so lost to his view in this perspective of life that his death becomes fused for him with his glory: "The hour has come . . . "—for what?— "for the Son of man to be glorified" (John 12:23). He is "the resurrection and the life." That is enough. He cannot die, and that approaching death is only the gateway to an imminent new life and to a glory that is increased by all that he will have suffered.

Our Gateway to a Full Life

The spirit in which Jesus walks toward death is also the one in which we who believe in him must go to meet death. The story of his cross and of his resurrection, forever inseparable, is renewed in us because Jesus dwells in us. There he accomplishes invisibly that which he accomplished visibly in himself so that he might serve as an example for all. Just as he could not go to take possession of his new life, either for himself or for his church, without passing through the cross, so we can find no other path for arriving at the full expression of the resurrection and the life that he communicates to us. "Flesh and blood cannot inherit the kingdom of God, nor does the perishable inherit the imperishable" (1 Corinthians 15:50). Though we carry that life within us, we are unable in our present state to receive it—I was going to say, to bear it—in all its fullness. We must be changed.

That change can take place without death, as it did in Moses and Elijah and as it will in those who are found alive when Jesus returns, but in the common order to which all others are subject, it takes place only through death. "For this perishable body must put on the imperishable, and this mortal body must put on immortality. When the perishable puts on the imperishable, and the mortal puts on immortality, then shall come to pass the saying that is written: 'Death is swallowed up in victory' " (1 Corinthians 15:53-54). From this comes the cry of the church, "O death, where is your victory? O death, where is your sting?" (1 Corinthians 15:55).

We Will Never Die

No, we will never die, just as Jesus could not die. We will never die because Jesus *cannot* die. What the world calls death, we call our sleep. We will not allow the uprooting of this name that Jesus gave for our death; a name that entirely changes its appearance. At the close of this day, you will not find yourself complaining at having to deliver yourself over to sleep. Nor, in the same way, do we complain at having to give ourselves over to sleep in Jesus at the close of an arduous and consuming career. Rather than dread its coming, it is during the interval that separates us from it that "we groan, longing to put on our heavenly dwelling. . . . For while we are still in this tent, we sigh, being burdened—not that we would be unclothed but that we would be further clothed, so that what is mortal may be swallowed up by life. . . . We know that while we are at home in the body we are away from the Lord. . . . We would rather be away from the body and at home with the Lord" (2 Corinthians 5:2,4,6,8).

To the world, this seems a generous illusion, but for the believer it is a blessed reality. It is a reality justified by countless facts in the early church, whose theology was not yet very systematic but whose faith was simple, and firm in proportion to its simplicity. Saint Paul, from whom we just borrowed those burning words of eternal life, wrote to the Philippians as something that went without saying, "For to me to live is Christ, and to die is gain. My desire is to depart and be with Christ, for that is far better" (Philippians 1:21,23). His was the voice of the church of his day, and with great simplicity he realized the truth of what Jesus said to those who are his: "Everyone who lives and believes in me shall never die."

Woe to us, inheritors of the faith of those first Christians, if we are not also the inheritors of their hope! Woe to us, above all, if we deal with death as the world does—a world that is estranged from Christ—thus giving the world room to doubt that the statement "Christ Jesus . . . abolished death and brought life and immortality to light" (2 Timothy 1:10) is anything more than a metaphor.

The Bread of Life

Christians, have you experienced in listening to me develop my text, what I experienced in meditating on it? Have you come to glimpse within faith in Jesus Christ a power, a grace, a light, and a deliverance that had never before been revealed to us there? How fortunate we are to believe in Jesus Christ, at least if the faith that is in us is really the kind to which the promises of my text are made! What jealous care we must take to be certain of that!

There is a faith, as easy as it is widespread, that consists of accepting evangelical doctrine without a struggle and that feels it needs nothing more than an orthodox profession as evidence of its existence. But the faith to which Jesus is appealing here is of a totally different sort. It is less a knowing than a having. It consists less in being acquainted with Jesus than in possessing him. It is not so much conveyed through man's teaching as it is created through the power of the Holy Spirit. It is not a new believing, it is a new life.

Among the varied images through which Jesus carefully portrays this faith in his effort to avoid all confusion, there is one that is stranger and more vivid than all the others. It appears to have been a particular scandal to the apparent disciples and a great lesson on salvation to the faithful disciples. It is the one that he gives as the basis of his discourse in Capernaum in the sixth chapter of Saint John. It is "the bread of life . . . that comes down from heaven, so that one may eat of it and not die. . . . If anyone eats of this bread"—and eats of it by faith—"he will live forever" (John 6:35,50-51). Soon he explains himself more clearly and more strangely still. "The bread that I will give for the life of the world is my flesh. . . . Whoever feeds on my flesh and drinks my blood has eternal life, and I will raise him up on the last day. For my flesh is true food, and my blood is true drink. . . . As the living Father sent me, and I live because of the Father, so whoever feeds on me, he also will live because of me" (John 6:51,54-55,57).

Let us not seek to probe the profound mystery of these words. Above all, let us not forget, just as he himself warned us, that his "words . . . are spirit and life" and that "the flesh is of no avail" (John 6:63). But having said all that, let us be honest. What an intimacy such a faith supposes between Jesus Christ and the believer! What a complete union of one with the other! What a profound difference between the believer and the one who does not believe!

Very well then, that living faith, that true faith, that created and creating faith, is it really yours? Lord, "increase our faith!" (Luke 17:5). "I believe; help my unbelief!" (Mark 9:24).

Resurrection Life and Communion

If this day of Easter seals the promise of my text through the resurrection of Jesus Christ and turns it into history, the communion to which we are invited brings it into view, placing it in our hands and before our eyes. For what does it show us if it is not that the One who gave his flesh and blood for us is also the One whose flesh and blood, when they are received by us as food and drink, will surely communicate his life and immortality to us? Therefore, open your hearts to receive your Savior who gives himself to you, and "bring them to him," according to that lovely expression in our confession of faith, "as empty vessels, so that he might send them back full of his grace and life." [6]

---

[6] This appears to be an allusion to, rather than a direct quote from, the 1559 French Confession of Faith (also known as the Confession of La Rochelle). The English translation of the text referred to, taken from volume 3 of Philip Schaff's *The Creeds of Christendom* 6th ed., 3 vols. (Grand Rapids, Mich.: Baker, 1996, reprinted by arrangement with Harper and Row), 381 is "All who bring a pure faith, like a vessel, to the sacred table of Christ, receive truly that of which it is a sign;" the resurrection life of Jesus Christ imparted to us.

Good communion does not give eternal life; that life is promised to faith, not to the sacrament. Yet communion nourishes faith by offering to it the simple, vivid, and rich picture of what Jesus is for our inner man. The sacrament will be all the more beneficial as it becomes more transparent. By this I mean that it will fade into the background in order to let Jesus Christ be seen. Thus the ideal sacrament would be one that has us so engaged with Jesus Christ that the sacrament itself is lost from view. Jesus gave that transparency to the sacrament of communion by the simplicity of the elements that he chose for it.

You, in turn, should give it back to him by "looking" without unbelief, without distinction, without division "to Jesus, the founder and perfecter of our faith" (Hebrews 12:2). Then you will receive this bread and wine as food for eternal life. Then you will recognize within yourselves that at this table you have found the one who is "the resurrection and the life."

Too Late!
(God Faithful in His Threats)

ುಾ

(Paris, 1854)

Luke 13:1-5

There were some present at that very time who told him about the Galileans whose blood Pilate had mingled with their sacrifices. And he answered them, "Do you think that these Galileans were worse sinners than all the other Galileans, because they suffered in this way? No, I tell you; but unless you repent[1], you will all likewise perish. Or those eighteen on whom the tower in Siloam fell and killed them: do you think that they were worse offenders than all the others who lived in Jerusalem? No, I tell you; but unless you repent, you will all likewise perish."

---

[1] The French version from which Adolphe Monod was quoting has "unless you are converted" in this passage, in place of the more usual "unless you repent." In each case a deep inward change of heart attitude resulting from a recognition of our sin is in view. Repentance is the gateway to conversion, but it is also the ongoing need of each Christian, as the Holy Spirit reveals new areas of sin in our lives.

Judgments Designed to Warn Us

My brothers, history teaches us nothing about the Galileans whom Pilate, a magistrate harsh to the point of cruelty, seems to have had slaughtered as they were celebrating a religious sacrifice. Nor does it tell us about the tower built in Jerusalem near the pool of Siloam, which had fallen, crushing eighteen persons beneath its debris. No matter. This affects neither Jesus' purpose in addressing his listeners nor my purpose in addressing you.

In the sudden destruction that surprised a few sinners in their security, in one case through the decision of power and in the other by a natural accident, Jesus wants his questioners to see judgments designed to warn all men through what happened to a small number of victims. He wants them to see God delivering the blows of his justice while making that justice serve the cause of his mercy. Far from considering themselves better than those who were just carried off by a sudden catastrophe, those who escaped should learn that a similar fate is reserved for them unless they are converted. Explained in this way, Jesus' warning is addressed to us no less than to his contemporaries.

Great God, God of justice, God of mercy, spare us! But whether you spare or whether you strike, cause us to be instructed so that we might be converted and in no wise perish!

"To Perish" and "To Be Converted"

To give a complete discourse on the matter at hand would require beginning with a clear definition of the two terms *to perish* and *to be converted*. As I am anxious to get to the practical application, I leave this double definition to your own care, relying on your good judgment and good faith. I offer only a few brief remarks.

To Perish: the Loss of Our Soul

Even though Jesus may well have had the imminent destruction of Jerusalem in view in proclaiming the words of my text, you will all agree that his thought doesn't end there. The punishment that he announces against the impenitent is, above all, the judgment to come, the loss of the soul.

What does that loss consist of? What does it mean *to perish*? To perish, according to Scripture—that is to say, according to God—is to live under "the LORD's curse" (Proverbs 3:33). It is to go "into the eternal fire prepared for the devil and his angels" (Matthew 25:41). It is to be delivered into the place "where their worm does not die and the fire is not quenched" (Mark 9:48). It is to wish we "had not been born" (Matthew 26:24). It is to cry out "to the mountains and rocks, 'Fall on us and hide us . . . from the wrath of the Lamb' " (Revelation 6:16). It is to inherit "the wrath to come" (Matthew 3:7) instead of eternal life.

As to the sense of these declarations, my dear listener, and specifically the length of those future punishments, I offer no commentary, no debate. I rely on you for that. If eternal punishment is not in the Scriptures, I don't want you to see it there; and if it is there, I want you to see it with your own eyes and not with mine. I offer only a simple question addressed to your sound judgment. Consider the language I just quoted and which is not mine but that of the prophets, the apostles, and Jesus Christ. Isn't it true that, no matter what the interpretation—and, once again, I leave to you the job of interpreting it for yourselves—there is something terrifying in this language beside which all the calamities of this present life are not worthy to be mentioned? Very well, that is enough for my present purpose.

To Be Converted: A Deep, Inward Change[2]

I won't dwell on this any further, and I rely equally on you as to the meaning of *to be converted*. You know it well enough; it isn't light that you lack. Conversion is an inner and profound change whose author is the Spirit of God, whose principle is faith in "Jesus Christ and him crucified" (1 Corinthians 2:2), and whose fruit is a new life. In a word, through conversion one becomes a real believer and a true saint.

Some among you—many among you, I like to believe—have experienced this change; a change which you should have no qualms about recognizing, provided that you give all the glory to God alone. But aren't there others who, by their own testimony, have experienced nothing of this nature? It is to them, it is to you, it is to each of you individually who judge yourselves not to have been converted that I address myself today. I want to ask you once, very seriously, what you do with the warning of my text. You hear Jesus Christ saying to you, "If you are not converted, you will perish." You say that you are not converted. You are exposed to death every day, and yet you live in tranquility. How can that be?

How Could You Doubt?

To that question there is only one possible answer: you do not take Jesus Christ's warning seriously. It's not that you reject the truth of Scripture or the authority of Jesus Christ. No, you are not irreligious. I don't even imagine that you are

---

[2] Although this sermon was particularly addressed to those who had, by their own admission, not been converted, its message is far broader. It is a good reminder to Christians not to gloss over sinful attitudes and actions for which we should repent. Just as importantly, this sermon should ignite in each of us a greater sense of urgency to reach the unconverted, be they among our friends and family or on the far side of the planet.

unbelieving. It is just that, through a contradiction that I can in no wise explain, you are unbelieving on one point. The promises of the gospel, fine. Its doctrines, fine again. But its warnings, and above all this terrible warning that deals with a mysterious future, no, you cannot subscribe to that without reservation; and reservation, once placed at the disposal of an unconverted sinner, extends itself with pleasing elasticity just as far as his comfort requires. "God's anger is only a figure of speech." "God is much too good to treat his creatures with such sternness." "Man is too weak to be judged as being so guilty." "Can someone be lost by doing what everyone else does, and can salvation be the exception?" "Besides, does it really rest with us to believe and be converted?" Is that not, my dear listener, at the heart of your thinking? Then I can respond to you with reasons, and with the very strongest reasons.

If God is good, he is also holy. His holiness requires a sanctioning of his law, and abandoning that sanctioning to the judgment of the self-interested sinner would be to make a mockery of it. Then, too, if one part of Scripture is brought into question, the rest will be also, and each person will end up retaining only that which suits his ideas, his tastes, or his needs. Finally, this is Jesus Christ who is speaking—he who is real truth, real holiness, and real love. Whom will you believe if you do not believe him?

The Answer of History

But I have an even shorter and more decisive answer: that of facts. If you don't want to judge what God will do in the future by the warnings he gives you, at least judge what he will do by what he has already done in the past, for it would be futile to maintain that God cannot do something that he has consistently done. More than once over the course of the centuries, God has given men threats similar to the one we are now considering. The only difference is that those dealt with the present life so that we can trace their accomplishment. Since most people refused to believe them, we need only see whether their hopes, founded on reasons similar to yours, were realized or disappointed. It is a question of history, and the answer is in the events.

Here in brief is that answer: God warns men of earlier ages just as he warns you; men of earlier times doubt the threat addressed to them just as you doubt the one addressed to you; and, when it is *too late* to take the warning seriously, experience justifies God's Word and not them, just as experience will justify God's Word and not you.

You might argue with me that God's past punishments visited on human unbelief are so different from the future punishments he has pronounced against final impenitence that we cannot conclude the reality of the latter from that of the former. That objection would be valid if I were preaching on justice or on the possibility of those future punishments. A temporal punishment is one thing, and a spiritual punishment is something else. Above all, a temporary punishment is one thing, and an eternal punishment is something else. But I am preaching on *God's faithfulness in his threats*, and I conclude that since events have always verified the threats he made in the past, whatever they might have been, so they will equally verify the threats he has made for the future, whatever they might be. (I use the phrase "whatever they might be" out of deference to you.)

My conclusion is perfectly legitimate and in harmony with the spirit of the Scriptures, especially since they portray those visible and transitory events to which I am appealing today as destined, in the divine plan, to serve as types and tokens of the invisible and eternal things in which all will come to an end. From this point of view, what I am quoting to you are more than examples. They are arguments; arguments framed expressly by God.

A Rare but Necessary Sermon Topic

But will you really understand my feelings as I present these terrifying images to you? It is almost a departure from my normal preaching style, which, as you well know, is so little concerned with this matter—perhaps too little concerned with it, perhaps less concerned with it than was the preaching of Jesus Christ and his apostles. Could this also represent a leaven of doubt on my part and a concession to the laxness of the century? Whatever the reason, this is one of the subjects that I deal with only at the price of doing violence to myself and because I am constrained to do so in the interests of your salvation. I readily speak on grace and pardon, but a faithful servant of Jesus Christ must do the one without neglecting the other.

The preaching of law and judgment may be even more necessary than usual at a time when all strong ideas are fading away, when feeling and character are getting ever more lax, and when God's mercy is assured of a warm welcome, provided that it is well divorced from his holiness. This is a fatal error that compromises mercy no less than holiness, for mercy assumes and is a measure of divine holiness, just as deliverance assumes and is a measure of man's peril. Whatever the case, God, like Jesus Christ, cannot be "divided" (1 Corinthians 1:13). We must either take him as he is or leave him alone.

Arguments From Genesis

Adam's Fall

First example. It is not long in making itself known. The world has scarcely been born. God had placed the man in Eden, telling him, "You may surely eat of every tree of the garden, but of the tree of the knowledge of good and evil you shall not eat, for in the day that you eat of it you shall surely die" (Genesis 2:16-17). For Adam, that threat didn't have the precise meaning that it has for us. What is death when one has known only life? Nevertheless, he must at least have understood that the punishment with which he was threatened was nothing less than the sudden destruction of all the bliss he enjoyed. That should have been enough to restrain him had he simply and naturally believed the threat of this God who had satisfied him with so many good things.

But here an unknown voice (alas, far too well known since then!) breathes in his ear that seductive hope: "You will not surely die. For God knows that when you eat of it your eyes will be opened, and you will be like God, knowing good and evil" (Genesis 3:4-5). And truly, using the kind of reflection that reassures you today, there was much to say against the accomplishment of the divine threat, without even having recourse to the serpent's impious hypothesis.

Whatever this predicted death might be, what rational connection could Adam imagine between it and the taking of a fruit—the only forbidden fruit among a thousand others that were permitted? How could that which everywhere else served to nourish man serve, in this case, to deprive him of life? Then, too, how could the loss of all God's gifts and even of life itself be commensurate with one single act of disobedience, and a small and insignificant one at that? Where is the Father who punishes his son to the point of death (see Proverbs 19:18; 23:13-14)? Finally, what a pretense for God to have created man only to destroy him. Would he not have abstained from forming him, or at least from forming him as a free being, rather than deliver him up almost defenseless, through the very tendencies he had put within him, to a temptation as alluring as its consequences are terrible?

God's wisdom, God's righteousness, God's goodness, all seemed to forbid taking his threat rigorously. And then there is the fairness brought up by his opponent, who had no apparent interest in deceiving the man and whose commentary seemed confirmed by the very name God gave to the fatal tree.

All these thoughts, which you should recognize as analogous to yours, filled the first woman as she "saw that the tree was good for food, and that it was a delight to the eyes, and that the tree was to be desired to make one wise" (Genesis 3:6), and as she stretched forth her hand toward it. Listen to the silence that extends throughout creation, suspended in anticipation of a terrible event. . . . It is done. The experiment has been tried. Eve has eaten, and Adam with her. Their curiosity has been satisfied; their eyes are open.

Very well, with those open eyes, how does God's threat appear? Was it true or wasn't it? Go and ask Adam kneeling beside the body of Abel, slain by Cain—calling to him, but no response—shaking him, but no awakening—gradually persuading himself that this, without doubt, is the death that God announced to him as the price of his sin. That death is not only real, since it has come, but it is more hideous than all his conceptions of it. That death is not only for him, it is for his entire race, with his sons sharing in it after him—or rather before him! That death is for him not only a physical death, it is a moral death, and the loss of one of the brothers is the crime of the other! That death is not only a future death, it is a present death, so that Adam standing full of life before the closed gate of Eden beholds the open gate leading to every suffering in this life—not to mention what he glimpses of the suffering reserved for the life to come.

He didn't want to believe before seeing. Now he is instructed by sight, but instructed *too late*, when no power on earth can restart the trial.

Now consider Adam as the tempter, henceforth unmasked, says to him again with a bitter sneer, "You will not surely die." Ask him what you should do with the threat addressed to you, which is just another form of the trial he faced. What would he say to you? What *could* he say to you, assuming he had not become a demon himself? What could he say except that you should believe the threat without hesitation or reserve? Alas, if he had done that himself, Abel would not be dead and Cain would not be a murderer!

THE FLOOD

Second example. Sixteen hundred years have passed since creation. God says to Noah, "I will bring a flood of waters upon the earth to destroy all flesh in which is the breath of life under heaven. Everything that is on the earth shall die. But I will establish my covenant with you, and you shall come into the ark, you, your sons, your wife, and your sons' wives with you" (Genesis 6:17-18). Noah, "herald of righteousness" (2 Peter 2:5), builds the ark and announces the coming judgment to his contemporaries more by his works than by his words. Meanwhile, "God's patience waited" (1 Peter 3:20). Thus one hundred and twenty years of mercy pass before the time fixed for justice, while the invincible unbelief of Noah's contemporaries turns that time into one hundred and twenty years of hardening. "They were eating and drinking and marrying and being given in marriage, until the day when Noah entered the ark" (Luke 17:27) and the door closed on him.

Here again, reasons to doubt are not lacking. First, the corruption of mankind doesn't appear to be what Noah wants to say it is. That "the wickedness of man was great in the earth" (Genesis 6:5), fine. But that "every intention of the thoughts of his heart was only evil continually" (Genesis 6:5), that is a clear exaggeration. And then, if it is true that this corruption is universal, that in itself is a sort of excuse. It must be natural and inevitable if it is common to the entire race without exception.

Besides, what is this flood of which we are to be afraid? Supposing the idea that God would come and submerge the newly created human species were credible, is it even possible? God can do all things, true; but still we must exclude that which is inherently contradictory. Has anyone ever seen waters, which always seek the lowest level, being raised up so as to cover the earth without leaving even the mountains as a refuge for its inhabitants? Isn't that contrary to the best known laws of nature and the good sense of a child?

And then, how do we know that it is God who said that to Noah? Noah is a good man, to be sure, but is he infallible? In any case, charity and humility are not among the virtues of one who damns the entire human species—except, of course, for himself and his family—and who presents all that to us as an inspiration from God! From God? And what kind of God? A God without dignity, who is capable of displeasure and vengeance; a God without foresight, who didn't know, in making man, that after several centuries he would repent of having formed him; a God without pity, who breaks with his hands the work of his hands and who, insensitive to the physical suffering and moral torture of thousands upon thousands of his creatures, annihilates all the families on earth in a single stroke—except for his eight favorites! And this should be the God who created us! The God upon whom Adam called! The God whom Abel worshipped! The God before whom Enoch walked!

This is all very well reasoned—just as well as you reason about the threat of my text—but while they are reasoning in this way, the flood comes and carries off the reasoning along with the reasoners. Or if some of them manage to reach the mountain tops, the water climbs up after them, as if gifted with life in order to pursue them. There is the last man, the sole survivor of the last family, as he feels his last refuge slip away from beneath him. His envious gaze falls, but falls *too late*, on the floating haven with the eight believers, carried along by the same element that erases everything else from under the heavens. Hurry. Go and ask him before he expires, who was right. Was it the prophet of God who said, "Everything that is on the earth shall die," or was it the logic, the feeling, the conscience, and everything else to which the ancient serpent had given a voice saying once again, "You will not surely die!"?

Sodom

Third example. Four centuries after the flood, two angels say to Lot in Sodom, "Have you anyone else here? Sons-in-law, sons, daughters, or anyone you have in the city, bring them out of the place. For we are about to destroy this place, because the outcry against its people has become great before the LORD, and the LORD has sent us to destroy it" (Genesis 19:12-14).

This time, the threat has something more admissible. It is only a matter of a city instead of a world, and a city so corrupt that no punishment would seem to exceed its crimes. Besides, the angels have legitimized their mission by the marvel they have already accomplished on the detestable inhabitants of Sodom. So many reasons to believe! Yes, but do you think that reasons to doubt are lacking for Lot's sons-in-law? Learn, instead, that such reasons are never lacking to someone who needs them and seeks them.

Above all, everyone can always find a refuge, an excuse for doubting the threat, under the comfortable and spacious cloak of that grand phrase, that magic phrase—so dear to all creation, if man had not so much abused it—God's goodness. God, whom the multitude has selfish reasons to call *the good God*, is not only too good to destroy a world; he is too good even to destroy a city. As for me, an inhabitant of that city, it is my world. And I would say the same thing about my household. If God can destroy a household, why not ten households, why not a city, why not a country, why not a world?

Do you think that the corruption of the city removes the benefit of that goodness? Again, why should that be? Once a certain degree of sin can be assured of impunity, why not a greater degree? Please mark out for me the precise limit where the corruption that can count on God's indulgence ends and where that which can only expect his justice begins.

And then, it is you who find the men of Sodom to be so wicked, but they are careful not to judge themselves so harshly. Clear-sighted as to the faults of others and blind to his own, that is natural man in every age. Do you think that the men of Sodom were indifferent to the sins of those who perished in the flood? No, no. But to confuse them with those people, what a crying injustice! It is easy to become indignant when it is against others, or to repent when it is on a neighbor's account. But when it is you yourself, when "you are the man" (2 Samuel 12:7), that is what shocks, that is what we cannot recognize without a stroke of grace like the one that illumined David before Nathan (see 2 Samuel 12:7-15).

There were even half-holy considerations that could reassure Lot's sons-in-law and their fellow citizens. Weren't they good friends with Abraham who had just armed his household to deliver them and their king from the hands of Chedorlaomer (see Genesis 14)? And who knows whether the holy patriarch, whom God has heretofore always answered, isn't standing on the mountain praying for Sodom in this moment of peril?

And suppose someone had told them how they would be destroyed. What does a rain of fire and sulfur mean? A flood—that can be conceived. There is water in abundance on earth. But a rain of fire and sulfur? Where would you find these elements in the air unless God wanted to create a new agent expressly for making it an instrument of his wrath, as if the ordinary forces of nature would no longer suffice for him against poor Sodom?

I am omitting lots of other reasons to feel secure; reasons that heaven or earth—or hell—might have furnished for them. Thus, incredibly, the one righteous family in Sodom, the only family the Lord has promised to spare, is also the only one to tremble before his judgments, and while Lot does not rest until the destroying angel has promised to spare Zoar, all the others, beginning with his own sons-in-law, think he is making fun of them. They, in turn, mock him, "eating and drinking, buying and selling, planting and building" (Luke 17:28).

Very well, unfortunate ones, mock! Prove that the threat is vain! "Eat and drink!" but what is that dark cloud spreading over your city and over the surrounding plain? Where is it coming from, that new rain, mixed with fire that consumes you and sulfur that snuffs out your voice? Stop your demonstrations for a moment while God provides his own.

Ah, when an "eternal fire" has swallowed you up and made you an example to the rest of the Canaanites (see Jude 7), if only they had eyes to see; when enough fire and sulfur has been found in the air and enough bitumen in the ground to renew completely the face of your region; when, instead of one threatened city, four have perished, along with all the countryside between them; when that fertile countryside has given way to an immense plain of water, which posterity will sometimes call the Lake of Asphalt because of the bitumen that saturates its waves, or the Dead Sea because it cannot sustain any living creature; when your ground has become the dread of the physical world, your crimes the dread of the moral world, and your very name the type of shame and infamy; then, though it is *too late* for you, may your folly at least teach future generations whether the threat was an illusion. May it show the true source of the voice that said to you, "You will not surely die," lest the likes of Sodom and Gomorrah earn the envy of Chorazin and Bethsaida (see Matthew 11:21-24, Luke 10:10-14)—I want to say, the envy of Bordeaux, of Marseille, of Lyon, or of Paris!

Arguments from Israel's History

Would you like a fourth example? I have already given you three without leaving Genesis, which I have far from exhausted. In each case we see God warning; man reassuring himself; the events verifying, even surpassing the threat. In each case, those who would only yield to experience, instead of walking by faith, are convinced by the events, but convinced *too late*. That pattern, except for differences in time, place, and circumstances, is the unchanging story of unregenerate humanity. It is especially the unchanging story of that set-apart people who seem to have been intended as a living example to all others of human unbelief undoing the work of divine faithfulness.

Old Testament History

The Israelites in the wilderness are warned that they will be deprived of Canaan's rest if they continue to "test the LORD," yet they test him one last time at the border of the Promised Land. As a result they are thrown back into the desert until the whole generation that left Egypt has perished there during forty years of exile; all except for the only two men of that entire nation who are found faithful (see Numbers 13-14).

The Israelites of the conquest are warned that their rest in Canaan will be changed into perpetual calamity if they ally themselves with its former inhabitants (see Deuteronomy 7:1-4), yet they ally themselves with those inhabitants from the first days of their residence there (see Joshua 9:3-15). As a result, they go from being God's favored people to the most unfortunate people on earth, exchanging one master and yoke for another over a period of four hundred years.

The Israelites of the royalty are warned that Jerusalem will be taken and the temple burned if they persevere in their idolatry, yet they persevere in their idolatry, filling Jerusalem with foreign gods. As a result they are surprised one day by the Babylonians who take their city, burn their temple, and lead them into captivity for seventy years.

But I leave all that aside in order to come to an example taken from the time of the New Testament and from the discourses of Jesus Christ.

The Fall of Jerusalem Predicted by Christ

The second Jerusalem, proud of its second temple, has replaced the gross superstition of earlier times with the more subtle but no less deadly superstition of the Pharisees. It has raised its hand against the faithful John the Baptist and against the Son of God himself. Then Jesus utters this prediction against it, and utters it while weeping (ah, if we but knew enough, as Jesus did, to put the weight of our tears into our warnings):

> For the days will come upon you, when your enemies will set up a barricade around you and surround you and hem you in on every side and tear you down to the ground, you and your children within you. And they will not leave one stone upon another in you, because you did not know the time of your visitation. . . . But when you see Jerusalem surrounded by armies, then know that its desolation has come near. Then let those who are in Judea flee to the mountains, and let those who are inside the city depart, and let

not those who are out in the country enter it, for these are days of vengeance, to fulfill all that is written. Alas for women who are pregnant and for those who are nursing infants in those days! For there will be great distress upon the earth and wrath against this people. They will fall by the edge of the sword and be led captive among all nations, and Jerusalem will be trampled underfoot by the Gentiles, until the times of the Gentiles are fulfilled. — Luke 19:43-44; 21:20-24.

Who believes that threat? Who could believe it? How could a city fall into the power of the enemy when it is surrounded by a triple enclosure of fortifications and defended by a population that is not only valiant but also angry and desperate? How could the Lord deliver up to the Gentiles the people he has kept for his possession, the city he has chosen as "the place of [his] throne" (Ezekiel 43:7), the house of which he said, "My eyes and my heart will be there for all time" (2 Chronicles 7:16), and the land that prophesy fixes as the setting for his blessed reign? How, and according to what new laws of history, would the Jews be dispersed among all the nations of the earth without losing their nationality; shaken, says the prophet, "among all the nations as one shakes with a sieve, but no pebble shall fall to the earth" (Amos 9:9)? How . . . ?

Alas, multiply the "how's" as much as you like; but here are all the unrealizable threats happening down to the last detail. Here is the impregnable city taken by an enemy so astonished at his own victory that he doesn't know how to explain it except by the intervention of some vengeful God. Here is the Lord rejecting his people; here is the temple reduced to ashes, Jerusalem trampled under foot, and the land of Israel devastated by the Gentiles. Here are the Jews dispersed among all the nations and bearing with them wherever they go the innocent blood that they have called down on their own head: "His blood be on us and on our children!" (Matthew 27:25). And yet everywhere, they are still distinct from the rest of men, preserving their language, their intonation, their morals, their appearance, their indestructible character; always ready to re-gather at the first signal in order to verify the promises of prophesy just as exactly as they have verified its threats.

Go and ask the first Jew who comes along whether God is faithful in his threats. Or perhaps his eyes are still covered by a veil that keeps him from discerning the crime that could draw upon the second Jerusalem a captivity that has already lasted eighteen centuries without having reached its end,[3] while idolatry itself only brought a captivity of seventy years on the first Jerusalem. If so, then don't ask him. Simply look at him. In each Jew who comes before your eyes, see a sure, living, and walking proof that the voice that said, "You will not surely die," is a lying voice. See a proof that if Jesus Christ said, "Unless you are converted, you will all likewise perish," then you will infallibly perish if you are not converted!

THE EXAMPLE OF YOUR FUTURE

As for my fifth and last example, it is you who are going to supply it to me. In all that we have just recalled—and to which it would be only too easy to add—we have found such a constant and uniform progression that there would be no risk of error in anticipating the event based on the prediction. Very well, just as I could have fearlessly told of the fall of Jerusalem prior to its happening based solely on the testimony of Jesus Christ's prophesy, so today I can also tell your own future story based solely on the testimony of Jesus Christ's threat. I

---

[3] That captivity finally ended with the reestablishment of the state of Israel roughly one hundred years after this sermon was preached.

imagine myself on the day after the great judgment, and I relate what will have happened to you who are hearing the warning of my text today and who delude yourselves with the vague hope that it will never be carried out.

YOUR STORIES

In the time when the testing of the human race was still going on (I am speaking after the judgment), there was, in the nineteenth century of the Christian era, on the tiny globe of the earth, in a city called Paris, men who gloried as Christians in their possession of God's Word and as Protestants in preserving it in all its purity. They read in the divine Book, "Unless you are converted, you will all likewise perish," but it was as if their eyes were prevented from seeing.

More than one servant of Jesus Christ urged them to listen to this serious appeal, but their words were lost in the air. One of them, in particular, on the fifteenth day of January in the year of our Lord 1854,[4] begged them to pay attention, but in vain. Like Adam, like Noah's contemporaries, like Lot's fellow citizens, like the Jews of Jerusalem, they preferred to give ear to the traitorous voice repeating century after century, "You will not surely die." The preacher told them, "God has spoken," but they replied within themselves, "Sure, but in what sense did he say it?" The preacher told them, "Nothing is clearer than his threat," but they replied within themselves, "Preaching is always obscure." The preacher told them, "See what happened to Adam, to Noah's contemporaries, to Lot's fellow citizens, to the Jews in Jerusalem," but they answered within themselves, "Things are quite different now!"

The preacher did what he could, but they went away, some saying, "That man spoke very well;" and others "This is

---

[4] That is the date on which this sermon was preached in Paris, in the Temple de l'Oratoire. [A.M.]

serious. We need to think about it again." Yet they stayed just as they were, right up until death came to surprise them in their impenitence. And now, there they are in "this place of torment" (Luke 16:28).

There is the wealthy man who amassed treasure for himself and was in no way rich toward God. He judged society to be in sufficiently good order if he preserved his advantages. He "feasted sumptuously" (Luke 16:19) like the man in the parable, who considered himself to be above reproach for not having acquired his fortune through iniquity but who knew neither repentance nor faith nor charity nor a life of renouncement and sacrifice. There he is, suffering and crying out to Abraham, "Father Abraham, have mercy on me, and send Lazarus to dip the end of his finger in water and cool my tongue, for I am in anguish in this flame" (Luke 16:24). But now it is *too late*.

There is the poor man who, absorbed in the trials of life, obstinately closed his ear to the voice so tenderly saying, "Come to me, all who labor and are heavy laden, . . . and you will find rest for your souls" (Matthew 11:28-29). Instead of entering into agreement with God who visited him, he murmured against God and men, dreaming of the overturn of society so that he might have a better place. There he is, having exchanged a miserable life for a still more miserable eternity. Today he understands the apostle's words, "Look not to the things that are seen but to the things that are unseen" (2 Corinthians 4:18), and he fervently wishes he could begin life's trial again. But now it is *too late*.

There is the worldly woman whose heart and conscience more than once spoke in agreement with the gospel, saying, "You need to be converted," but she couldn't make up her mind to break with a world that showered her with praise or with a society of which she was the idol. There she is, and you can see what kind of world she is in; you can see what kind of society she is with! Oh, what would she not give today to find herself once again on the day when that minister of God urged her to "flee from the wrath to come" (Matthew 3:7). Then there was still time, but now it is *too late*.

THERE IS STILL TIME

Too late: bitter word, hellish word, word that is hell! *Too late*: which is to say, heaven become as brass and falling on us with all its weight! *Too late*: which is to say, the burning fire that burns, burns again, and is not extinguished; the gnawing worm that gnaws, gnaws again, and that alone will not die! *Too late*: which is to say God's mercy exhausted by his righteousness, restrained by his integrity, and no longer able to show itself in any direction without rending one of God's perfections. *Too late*: which is to say the despair of *I cannot* coupled with the bitterness of *I could have but didn't want to!* Too late . . .

But it is not *too late* for you who are listening to me! This is not history that I just gave in my last example! It is prophesy! Show it to be wrong, as the Ninevites did to Jonah's prophesy. You can do it! For you it is still daytime. For you God is still speaking. For you grace is still available. Yes, for you the Savior's arms are still open and seem to be extended on his cross only to welcome you. Ah, if you have previously doubted, doubt no more in front of that cross. Woe to the one who could coldly discuss the value of a threat that truth drags from a crucified Savior!

Take that threat by faith based on God's testimony alone, without waiting for the testimony of experience—that testimony for which one never waits without being lost. Take that threat such as it is, without your commentaries and without mine; take it terrible as it is but true as it is, merciful as it is—it only troubles you in order to save you! Take that threat quite simply, quite naturally, like a child, being less afraid of exaggerating it than of softening it, and watching out for anything that in any way resembles the incessant hissing of the ancient serpent, "You will not surely die!" Take that threat without worrying yourselves about the means for being converted; if your heart is right, you will find them. Only go, and God will direct you.

Above all, ah, take that threat based on the word of the "God" who "is love" (1 John 4:8,16), not as a threat of his anger but as a warning of his love, as a cry from his fatherly heart. It is a sign to you of all the help and deliverance that you will draw from the inexhaustible treasure of his compassion. "As I live, declares the Lord GOD, I have no pleasure in the death of the wicked, but that the wicked turn from his way and live; turn back, turn back from your evil ways, for why will you die, O house of Israel?" (Ezekiel 33:11).

"Today, if you hear his voice, do not harden your hearts" (Psalm 95:7-8, Hebrews 3:15, 4:7). Today, while God is speaking to you—God, I say, and not I. I have said nothing that I have not drawn from his Word. Today, while you live, while you can, while you want to. Today and not tomorrow. Do I have to tell you all my thoughts? In all likelihood, today— or never!

How many will there be in this gathering who will profit from this discourse? I don't know; God knows. But may there be at least one, and may it be you! Amen.

ଓଃ *part three* ଓଃ
Trust in the Lord

(Proverbs 3:5)

ଓଃ part three ଽ଼

Maturity in the Christian life comes slowly. Our first dazzling exposure to God's love, the early joy of a life made whole, the peace of a new set of priorities—these experiences can take us only so far. Do we, can we, still love and trust God when our plans go awry, our expectations are unfulfilled, or our health fails? Since August 1975, I have been learning, as countless Christians before me have learned, that it is most often in the hard times that growth happens. It is there, if we are teachable, that we slowly, gradually learn to trust God—really trust him—with one area of our lives after another. It is there that we learn to accept God's will for us as "good, and acceptable, and perfect" (Romans 12:2) and to embrace it as our own. These are not matters of a moment, but of a lifetime, and in the next sermon, "Embracing God's Plan," Monod treats them in a way that will challenge and comfort us all.

Over the years, I have also been learning about the true nature of the Christian's peace and joy, the subject of the final sermon, "The Happiness of the Christian Life." It is, to be sure, first and foremost the joy of having a Savior and being freed from the guilt and power of sin. It is the joy of communion with God. But it is also the inner peace that comes from submitting to the authority and wisdom of Scripture. It is the sense of wholeness and purpose that comes from having God as the central focus of all aspects of our lives. It is the joy of loving and serving others out of love for our Savior, loving them with a love that he supplies.

— *CKW*

EMBRACING GOD'S PLAN

ಜ

(Paris, 1850)

Jeremiah 10:23

I know, O LORD, that the way of man is not in himself, that it is not in man who walks to direct his steps.

Parallel texts:[1]

The steps of a man are established by the LORD, when he delights in his way. — Psalm 37:23

The heart of man plans his way, but the LORD establishes his steps. — Proverbs 16:9

A man's steps are from the LORD; how then can man understand his way? — Proverbs 20:24

---

[1] In meditating on his material, a preacher sometimes recognizes passages of Scripture suitable for confirming or clarifying the one that serves as his text, but that he finds no opportunity to develop in his discourse. These are the passages that I list under the heading of *Parallel texts*. [A.M.]

Our Frustrated Plans

The Bitterness of Frustration

Next to the weakness of the flesh that keeps us from accomplishing God's holy law (see Romans 8:3), there is nothing quite so bitter in life as our powerlessness to accomplish, by our own willpower, the plans that we have conceived. Perhaps this regret over our inability to do what we desire is even more poignant than our repentance for failing to do what we should. Regret has a less precise and less moral character than repentance, thus leaving the gospel less of a toehold either to reveal the wrong or to correct it. One can ponder with peace (though a peace tinged with pain and love) the sins of his life atoned for by the sacrifice of the cross, without having resigned himself to a thwarted career, unused natural gifts, ruined hopes of fortune, or perhaps simply to an alliance[2], a job, or a favor that he has sought in vain.

The bitterness of this regret is not only in the value we attach to the objects of our unfruitful pursuit. It is also, it is above all in the very sterility of the pursuit itself. For a spirit such as ours, capable of firm resolve and vigorous action, there is cruel disappointment in seeing even our most praiseworthy plans run aground; in finding a rock of Sisyphus in nearly every stone, great or small, that we strain to role up the side of the mountain.[3]

At last, having been taught by sad experience, man begins to doubt himself. This is the greatest humiliation and, at the same time, the greatest misfortune we can know, for

---

[2] This word can also be translated marriage.
[3] Sisyphus is a figure in Greek mythology whose eternal punishment in Hades was to push a heavy boulder up the side of a steep mountain only to find, on reaching the top, that it immediately rolled back to the foot of the slope.

confidence is the condition of strength. Just as unshakable faith in success produces all kinds of powerful men, so despair of success produces the weak and timid men who fill society, and—I wish I didn't have to add—the weak and timid Christians who encumber the church.

A Core of Peace and Hope

Very well, here in our text is a great thinker, a great saint, a great prophet who shares our sense of impotence, but who shares it in order to elevate it. Rather than simply deploring this helplessness as something that is, Jeremiah at the same time recognizes it as something that must be: "I know, O LORD, that a man's life is not his own; it is not for man to direct his steps." *I know*, literally *I have known*—there is the language of reflection. *O LORD*—there is the intonation of prayer. For Jeremiah, the inability that troubles you is a truth known from experience and faith. It is not that this truth isn't mixed with bitterness for him, too. In fact, it appears to him in the midst of bitterness, springing from the warnings God puts in his mouth against his fellow citizens.[4]

As he sees Judah's tent destroyed and Judah's children being led captive (Jeremiah 10:20), as he hears the sound of the enemy's feet descending from the land of the north to

---

[4] Jeremiah here displays the double relationship of the prophet, which seems to reflect the double nature of the Son of God, the prophet of prophets. Jeremiah represents God before his people at the same time that he represents his people before God. That is why we see him, in turn, so identifying himself with the God who speaks through him that he espouses his righteous vengeance, and then so identifying himself with the people who are his flesh and blood that he sees himself suffering all the evils with which he threatens them. Out of this, a marvelous dialogue arises where the speaker changes, without any indicated transition, from the one who strikes to the one who is stricken (verse 18 to verses 19-20; verses 21-22 to verses 23 and 25), so that Jeremiah sometimes disappears before the God whom he announces and sometimes before the people whom he personifies. [A.M.]

reduce Judah's cities to a wasteland (Jeremiah 10:22), Jeremiah at first personifies his entire people in his laments. "My wound is grievous. But I said, 'Truly this is an affliction, and I must bear it'" (Jeremiah 10:19). After that he stops, as if pulling himself together, and collects his thoughts into this more tranquil expression of his deep dejection: "I know, O LORD, that the way of man is not in himself, that it is not in man who walks to direct his steps" (Jeremiah 10:23).

But through the dejection, do you not discern a core of peace and hope? This God who holds us between his hands is a God filled with a mercy that permeates even his harshest judgments against his own people. Thus the holy prophet rests in the sense that it is God who guides us and not we ourselves. He rests there even under the blows from his rod, a rod which is stern but always fatherly for those who wait on him. "Correct me, O LORD, but in justice; not in your anger, lest you bring me to nothing" (Jeremiah 10:24).

Jeremiah, like David and Solomon,[5] is a faithful prophet, whose personal life and suffering bring together experiences that are instructive for all mankind. Thus he transmits to future races, as a combined token of humiliation and encouragement, the heavenly maxim: *In this life, man accomplishes not his own plan, but that of God, which always triumphs in the end.* Let us study this thought in greater depth.

THE MISSING ELEMENT

As an intelligent and responsible creature, I know how to propose a goal and to set about attaining it. Thus I make plans for the development of my abilities, for the choice of my career, for the education of my family, for the running of my household. But though I can will and act, I cannot arrange either circumstances or events or myself as I would

---

[5] See the parallel texts on page 155. [A.M.]

like. If my plans sometimes succeed, often, most often, they run aground. This inherent weakness in my actions speaks of some missing element whereby my real life is in painful contrast to my ideal life.

God's Hidden Plan

It is at this moment that Jeremiah intervenes to uncover for me, in the disorder of my plan, an order corresponding to a better plan, God's plan for me. It is a perfect plan, which is of greater value than mine, whether for the general interests of society or for my personal interests. It is a powerful plan, which is infallibly accomplished whatever the fate and vicissitudes of mine might be. It is a controlling plan—if you will allow me to put it that way—which sovereignly dominates mine and which, if necessary, corrects it. Thus what is called a setback in my plan, takes on the name of success in God's plan.

This is almost like a tapestry scene that is worked from the back. The colored threads that the workman weaves with a gentle hand offer only an inextricable confusion to the eye until they are viewed from the true side, the side of the artist. Man's plan is only the back of life's tapestry, while God's plan is the front.

Seen from this vantage point, my action is never without order or without fruit, for I always accomplish God's plan, whether I know it or not and, beyond that, whether I want to or not. When I walk in harmony with God, I succeed, and I accomplish his plan, even while thinking, perhaps, that I am only accomplishing my own. If I walk in opposition to him, I fail, but I still accomplish his plan, even in the reversal of my own. For lack of serving him through my obedience, I serve him by my very disobedience, "for all things are [his] servants" (Psalm 119:91).

Man's Activity and God's Sovereignty

Are we then quietists or fatalists? Are we quietists? Do we, under the pretext that God can do all that he wishes, repudiate man's action and ask that he wait with folded arms for the divine plan to develop? Far from it! There is much that man can do; probably more than any of us has ever achieved or imagined. Letting go would thus be to abandon our most glorious privilege and our holiest obligations. But, through a mystery that we can never penetrate to its depths in this life, human action has free reign within the vast bosom of the divine will. This will shelters it and—if I dare to say so—respects it even while controlling it.

Well then, are we fatalists? Do we, under the cloak of God's sovereign ordering of the universe, deny man's liberty, with the moral responsibility that stems from it? Still less! To deny man's liberty, to suppose that he is constrained in his disobedience—or even in his obedience—would be to overthrow the basis of all morality, of all religion, and most especially of the Christian religion. But through a second mystery that is even more impenetrable than the first, human liberty is allied with divine sovereignty without losing its own identity. This divine sovereignty contains it without constraining it and directs it without determining it.

Let us probe no deeper into this double problem, which philosophy has always found to be insoluble and which Scripture itself leaves unresolved. All we can do is to note as coexisting facts, contrary as they may seem, man's real action and God's omnipotence, man's full liberty and God's absolute sovereignty. Moreover, it is a glorious enough prerogative for a created being to have been made capable of will and duty, without pretending that his derived initiative absorbs the creative initiative from which it springs.

Whatever the case, I find myself depending simultaneously on two plans whose secret relationship escapes me:

God's plan and my own plan. But the first of these is infallibly brought to pass, either with the other or without it or against it. It always dominates the second without ever crushing it. This cannot be expressed more concisely or more accurately than Solomon did: "The heart of man plans his way, but the LORD establishes his steps" (Proverbs 16:9).

EXAMPLES FROM EXPERIENCE

Experience will serve to clarify this profound doctrine. The history of nations, of great men, and of everyday life all equally reveal to the attentive observer a plan from God that determines all things without violating man's freedom of action.

NATIONS OR PEOPLE: THE EXAMPLE OF ROME

Of all nations, the one that would furnish me with the most decisive example is the Israelites. God's direction in their history is rendered both more tangible than elsewhere through the covenant he made with them, and more visible through the revelations of his Word. Their story shines equal light on their freedom, which they seldom use except to transgress the designs of heavenly mercy, and on God's Sovereignty, which uses them, even on the day of Golgotha, "to do whatever [his] hand and [his] plan had predestined to take place" (Acts 4:28).

But to take a less frequently cited example, let's consider the astonishing city that has served both as the political center of the ancient world and the religious center of the modern world. If ever a plan belonging to man has appeared, it would be in pagan Rome extending its network of political domination from one people to another, or in Christian Rome extending the more subtle network of religious domination from one church to another. And yet, when one looks more closely, one clearly discovers in all that happened, in both pagan Rome and Christian Rome, the marks of a plan that was not born of man's mind but that takes its starting point and its strength from a higher plane.

Each plan had been working itself out for centuries before it began to reveal itself—or rather to impose itself— on the men whose mission it was to recognize or proclaim it. Half of the world was under the power of Rome before Julius Caesar dreamt of making it the master of the other half; likewise for the church and Gregory VII. It was only the sight of what had already been done that was able to suggest, even to the ambition and genius of these two men, the thought of what was left to do.

The men didn't make the plan, the plan made the men. These men simply had the glory of intelligently obeying a direction that many others had followed without understanding it. With still greater intelligence, they would have restated, each in his own way, what Jeremiah says in my text. "I know, O LORD, that the way of man is not in himself, that it is not in man who walks to direct his steps."

GREAT MEN: THE EXAMPLE OF MOSES

Now, let us narrow the field of our observation. Let us ponder one of those men whom the world honors with the name of *great* because of the enduring mark they leave on earth after they are gone. Remove from a great man his country, his era, his education, his surroundings—all the things that do not depend on him—and you remove all the essential elements of his greatness.

Consider the example of Moses, the first man in religious history whom we know well. What is freer, more energetic, more individual than Moses coming to grips first with king of Egypt, whose wrath he defies, then with Israel, whose stubborn resistance he overcomes, then with the desert, whose sterility he makes fertile, then with heaven itself, whose vengeance he disarms. Moses is a multi-faceted man—at once ruler, prophet, priest, liberator, provider, legislator, reformer, and founder of a new people. And what a people! And in what a time!

But do you think that the plan Moses executed was his own? Ah, who could attribute such a plan to a man's own spirit without folly or ungodliness? It was so little from Moses that when God first proposed it to him, Moses began by obstinately refusing, excusing himself based on his natural timidity and his speech impediment.[6] Moses' plan was and could only be from this God who, before proposing it to Moses, had prepared Moses throughout the first two thirds of his life to accomplish it. Eighty years of education for forty years of activity—"is this the manner of man" (2 Samuel 7:19 KJV), or is it the manner of one who, in the apt words of a church father, "is patient because he is eternal"?

Moses is brought up in the palace of the same Pharaohs from whose yoke he is to deliver his people. There, placed in daily contact with the double power of the kings and priests against whom, in God's time, he is to battle, Moses is instructed for a career of which he knows nothing.[7] That is the first forty years, and quite likely (see Acts 7:25) it is at the end of this time that he begins to get a hint of his mission. Then after a brief visit with his brothers, he goes off to add to the forty years spent learning from Egypt, another forty years spent in studying the desert, guiding Reuel's flocks over the same paths where he must one day guide the Lord's flocks (see Isaiah 63:11 etc.).

It is on one of these nomadic excursions, it is at the foot of Mount Sinai, it is having arrived at the age of eighty, that

---

[6] "Now the man Moses was very meek, more than all people who were on the face of the earth" (Numbers 12:3). [A.M.]

[7] "Moses was instructed in all the wisdom of the Egyptians, and he was mighty in his words and deeds" (Acts 7:22). [A.M.]

Moses learns at last the goal of his past life. Perhaps he thought he was nearing the end of his career, lamenting not having been able to use it for his people. Yet now he learns that his past life has prepared him for the people of Israel, for Egypt, for the desert, for everything—everything except Canaan, where God knew he would never enter. Ah, when Moses goes to sleep in God within sight of that same Canaan after the forty years of his true work are accomplished, with what heart do you imagine he will have said in his last prayers, "I know, O LORD, that the way of man is not in himself, that it is not in man who walks to direct his steps"?

EVERYDAY LIFE: THE EXAMPLE OF RAISING A SON

Let us draw closer still. Let us come to our common everyday life, and to the aspect of it that is most intimately bound up with our person and our actions. What real part do you play in the arrangement of your domestic life? To begin at the beginning, how many aspects of even the most harmonious marriages escape not only from man's control but even from his expectations? Life, health, family, resources, or, beyond that, mutual sympathy and tenderness — how many things do they depend on that, in turn, scarcely depend on our wills any more than does "the lot . . . cast into the lap," whose "every decision is from the LORD" (Proverbs 16:33)? But let's stop at that which depends most on our wills: the education of our children.

Here is a son who has just been born to me. After God, I exert the greatest power in the world over him, materially, intellectually and spiritually. One would think that he would become what I want him to be, apart from the unexpected. Yes, apart from the unexpected; but that restriction goes a long way! Let us assume, however, a model upbringing such as you or I would dream of on the day when God gives us our first child. Activity, faithfulness, prudence, work, sacrifices, godliness, prayer, examples—nothing has been lacking. Even then, how many conditions over which you have no control must come together for the successful development of this son who is the object of so much love and concern!

His health: A delicate constitution, a poorly formed build, a thin voice, poor hearing or vision—there is enough to hinder all your plans. His intellectual faculties: A certain measure of ability is necessary for every work, and not everyone has that measure. Your child, forcing himself to please you, will perhaps languish over a task to which you have condemned him until the day when, belatedly convinced of your error, you let him follow his proper calling. His moral dispositions: Instead of a child who wishes but cannot, you have a child who can but will not; a lazy "son who brings shame" (Proverbs 10:5). You exhaust all the paths of warning, pleading, exhorting, and punishment on him, but without fruit. The fruit, if you are faithful, will come in God's time (see Proverbs 22:6), after God has made you see that he alone is God.

And what of his life? Truly, I was forgetting his life; his life, alas, perhaps cut off in the bud, just when his training begins, or, doubly alas, cut off in the flower, just when his education ends. And what of opportunity, of surroundings, of example, of companions, of teachers, of fortune, of location, of the spirit of the age, of the legislation of the land, of the organization of public education? There is no one on earth better instructed to repeat the lesson of Jeremiah than the father of a large family, entering, like Moses, into his rest in the presence of that unknown Canaan where the succeeding generation ventures. "I know, O LORD, that the way of man is not in himself, that it is not in man who walks to direct his steps."

Man Proposes and God Disposes

Thus the maxim of our prophet has in turn been proclaimed by the Scriptures, reconciled with healthy philosophy, traced through the course of human experience, and, I might add, passed into the popular saying, "Man proposes and God disposes." Henceforth, it appears to us that this maxim is without possible argument and with no other obscurity than that which dwells at the heart of all great moral questions. Human plans are dominated by a divine plan that is accomplished in a person's life without violating either his effective will or, above all, his moral freedom.

But there is little advantage to having established this doctrine if we don't show the use that a Christian should make of it in the conduct of his life. This will be the object of the remainder of this discourse, whose vibrant main point we are just reaching. May God's Spirit help us!

Entering Into God's Plan

The Christian has no simpler nor, at the same time, safer means for entering into the spirit of a revealed doctrine than to contemplate it put into practice by "Jesus Christ . . . come in the flesh" (1 John 4:2). Jesus is the model man, in whom all the great invisible truths are clothed with a visible body and receive the breath of life. Therefore it is in him that we must seek—or, rather, that we must observe—how we should apply Jeremiah's maxim

For Jesus, Two Plans Become One

No one else has more completely lived out the thought of my text than Jesus. No one else has more perfectly conformed himself to the divine plan. Jesus does nothing and can do nothing on his own (John 8:28; 5:30). He doesn't proclaim his own doctrine but the doctrine of the Father who sent him (John 7:16). He doesn't seek his own glory but the glory of the Father who sent him (John 7:18; 8:50). He doesn't accomplish his own will, but the will of the Father who sent him (John 5:30). He says only those things that the Father has said to him; he does only those things that Father has commanded him to do (John 8:28-29,38; 12:49-50, etc).

In addition, no one else has been more visibly prepared by God for the execution of a divine plan. Jesus' tribe, his family, his birth, Bethlehem and his star, the shepherds and the magi, the flight to Egypt and the withdrawal to Nazareth, the baptism of John and the temptation in the wilderness—all is arranged by the Father's hand. There is not a trace of human preparation or human plan in the life of Jesus.

And yet, in no one else has either man's will or his liberty shone forth more clearly than in Jesus. The same plan, which just appeared to us as belonging only to the Father who conceived it, appears to us equally as belonging only to the Son who executes it. From beginning to end, from before his birth until after his death, Jesus does nothing he does not want to do. If he is born into the human race, it is because he wanted to be. "Though he was in the form of God, . . . [he] made himself nothing, taking the form of a servant, being born in the likeness of men" (Philippians 2:6-7). If he dies as a man, it is because he wanted to. "Being found in human form, he humbled himself by becoming obedient to the point of death, even death on a cross" (Philippians 2:8). What's more, if he is resurrected from the dead, it is because he wanted to be. "I lay down my life that I might take it up again. No one takes it from me, but I lay it down of my own accord. I have authority to lay it down, and I have authority to take it up again" (John 10:17-18). And this testimony, which is the most striking that he has given of his own power, he ends—amazing thing!—with these seemingly contradictory words: "This charge I have received from my Father" (John 10:18).

Only one solution to this problem is possible. If the Son accomplishes his Father's plan and his personal plan all at the same time, it is because the two plans are really only one. It is because the Son has so fully adopted the Father's plan that he has made it his own. It is a plan which he seems, in turn, to have either accepted or chosen, depending on whether we look on him in his obedience or in his freedom. Through it he accomplishes the law of human nature that Jeremiah revealed in my text, but he does so in a way that robs it of all sense of weakness or even of necessity. The freer he is, the more obedient he becomes; and the more obedient he is, the freer he becomes.

Go and Do Likewise

There is the secret we were seeking; "Go, and do likewise" (Luke 10:37). Of these two plans before you, God's and your own, make only one. And since you can't impose your plan on God, adopt his, not in a spirit of servile constraint but in that of filial devotion.

Is it a question of the things that depend on you? Do only what you have reason to believe conforms to God's plan. In choosing a career, instead of asking what promises you the greatest success, well being, or influence, ask above all what God has marked out for you through your abilities, your training, your circumstances, or those inner callings that impress themselves on the faithful soul. In forming a partnership,[8] instead of asking what would best flatter your views of ambition, your projects for wealth, or your self-will, ask above all what will lend you the surest support for growing in the life of God and for accomplishing the work

---

[8] The same word can also be translated "marriage."

that he has given you to do on this earth. In the education of a child, instead of asking what is the direction advised by common practice, opinion, vanity, or interest, ask above all what best enters into the directions God has given you through health, abilities, leanings, or position.

Is it a question of the things that do not depend on you? Leave it to God, and may your peace come from telling yourself that his plan takes care of everything. It is his alone to measure the share of joys and sorrows that is appropriate for you. As to the sweet things, the consolations that God has reserved for you, take them, savor them, even the smallest of them, and do so with a heart that is all the happier and more grateful for having gathered them from the Father's hand. But those that he has denied you, even the most desired and desirable of them, turn them into a sacrifice, and content yourself with the knowledge that it is that same Father's hand that has taken them from you. On the other side, when it comes to the privations and bitter things that God spares you, don't envy those "blessed who remained steadfast" in suffering (James 5:11), and if you go seeking after them, be fearful of giving way beneath a burden of your own choosing. But those that he has sent you, even if they should hinder your dearest, most useful, most beneficial projects, accept them as healthy exercises, suitable for your spiritual training and mercifully measured according to what you can bear.

Simply put, you need to know what plan God has formed for you, and, having found it, you need to adopt it as your own, as you saw Jesus do.

Discerning God's Plan

Please don't tell me that you are at a loss to discern God's plan. This discernment is promised to the simplicity of an upright heart. When a faithful soul is humbly pierced with the thought, "A man's steps are from the LORD; how then can man understand his way?" (Proverbs 20:24), and when he prays, "Make me know the way I should go . . . for you are my God" (Psalm 143:8,10), then the Lord answers him, "I will instruct you and teach you in the way you should go; I will counsel you with my eye" (Psalm 32:8).

The fact that Jesus has no plan other than God's is sufficient for that plan to be revealed to him—or rather, to be unfolded before him—day after day, and for the path of good works that God has prepared for him to be traced out, step by step. Sometimes this happens through an appeal addressed to him, sometimes through an event that takes place, sometimes through an inward impression, and sometimes through the material or spiritual necessities of life, yet it is all with so much openness and ease that the very question that preoccupies you doesn't even seem to pose itself to him.

Have his spirit, and you will have his light. Nature, men, events—all things will be to you like a divine course of instruction, where the faithfulness that gives will be measured according to the faithfulness that receives. If it enters into your Father's plans to hide the understanding of his designs from you for a time, as if to tenderly compel you to cling more closely to him, recall that what is important, after all, is not so much discerning God's plan as following it. God has ways of making us follow his plan even without making us discern it. "By faith Abraham obeyed when he was called to go out to a place that he was to receive as an inheritance. And he went out, not knowing where he was going" (Hebrews 11:8), but God knew, and that was enough. Walk likewise by faith, and if you want only his ways for your ways and his thoughts for your thoughts (see Isaiah 55:8), God will guide you even in the darkest of days.

The Results

When you walk thus by faith, you will simultaneously accomplish both God's plan, which has become yours, and your plan, which is united with his. This will be for you as it was for Jesus, the basis of a perfect reconciliation between seemingly opposing interests. On the one hand, by accomplishing God's plan you will have a sense of order, while on the other hand, by accomplishing your own plan you will have a sense of freedom. This is worth stopping to consider for a few moments, since it is nothing less than the simple yet profound solution to one of the greatest moral problems that has ever preoccupied human consciousness.

Order and Peace

You will have a sense of order because you will accomplish a plan that is from God and not from you. Suppose, on the contrary, that you could fully and invariably carry out a plan that came from you and not from God. Even then—I should perhaps say, especially then—what disorder! In the end, we cannot hide the fact that we are finite creatures who only see a few steps in front of us and who cannot consider anything within the full sweep of time and circumstance. You would be forever trembling for fear of mistaking the apparent interest for the real, the passing for the permanent, the visible for the invisible, the small for the great. You would not know how to decide between the risks of action and the perils of inaction. In the end, you would find rest only in completely unburdening yourself onto someone who knows the future as well as the present, the totality as well as the detail, the depths of things as well as the surface. In other words, you would find no rest except in the situation that exists today.

God's vast plan has the resources of the entire universe to support it, infinite space in which to unfold itself, and everlasting time for its development. Thus nothing is ever irreparable in it, nothing is hopeless, nothing is unforeseen, nothing is even compromised.

Instead of wearing ourselves out in sterile efforts at painting the beauty of this doctrine, let us rather look at it in Jesus, in the life in which it is transformed into history. What life has been more dominated, more permeated, and, alas, more torn by God's plan than that of Jesus? But where can we find a deeper or more constant sense of order and peace than in "Jesus Christ and him crucified" (1 Corinthians 2:2)? It is enough for the beloved Son to know that the Father's merciful plans are being carried out in his person. If it is part of the Father's plan to make him suffer as no man has ever suffered, he is sustained by telling himself, "For this purpose I have come to this hour" (John 12:27). The words that he spoke at the end, "I . . . accomplished the work that you gave me to do" (John 17:4), explain it all. What does it matter that he dies on a cross, that he dies in the prime of life, that he dies without having strengthened his disciples, that he dies without finishing his work? It isn't *his* work that he came to do, it is the work of his Father, and that work has been accomplished or the Father wouldn't withdraw him yet.

From a human perspective, what dies with Jesus is the salvation of the world, it is the foundation of the kingdom of heaven, it is prophesy verified, it is the serpent crushed, it is the reestablishment of everything. But that which dies doesn't die; instead, all those seeds are hidden only to be placed in the bosom of the Father, which, like fertile soil, will give them back with interest. The hour of the cross, the hour of upheaval, confusion and darkness in the domain of human plans is the hour of order, harmony and deliverance in the domain of the divine plan. "It is finished" (John 19:30).

Liberty and Life

But if there is no peace except in order, there is also no life except in liberty. Very well then, in the type of conduct you find taught in my text and in Jesus' example, you will at the same time feel at liberty, because even while you are accomplishing God's plan you will also be accomplishing your own plan, which you have conformed to his. This isn't absolute liberty, I agree, but it is all the liberty to which the creature can pretend. Absolute liberty consists of accomplishing what one wants, without being regulated by anyone and without giving account to anyone. It belongs only to God. The unique liberty of which we are capable consists of placing that divine liberty in our interests. It will be against us if we pursue an independent plan and for us if we hold fast to God's plan.

If the subordination of our plan to his could be perfect and the conformity of our will to his could be complete, then nothing more would be needed for us to be as infallible in our designs as God himself is. This is expressed in Jesus Christ's profound thought, "If you abide in me, and my words abide in you, ask whatever you wish, and it will be done for you" (John 15:7).

The Life of a Son

This promise comes from the most intimate depths of the gospel. God has made a covenant with us, not as a master with his slave, but as a father with his son; a son whom he doesn't subject to his plans but associates with them. It is as a son that Jesus adopts God's designs for him and that he invites us to adopt his designs for us. As a son; there is the key to the puzzle, for it is at once a word of submission and of love. As a son; one with the Father, and all the more in his own nature and spirit as he is more in the Father's nature and spirit. As a son; that is enough for dependence to fuse with liberty.

Has there ever in this world been a life more docile, more submitted, more acquiescent to God's plan than the life of Jesus? But has there ever in this world been a life more personal, more individual, more free? He is all the more himself for being more united with the Father, and—dare I say it?—he is all the more man for being more God. Thus, in his own person, Jesus resolves the problem of boundless liberty through unreserved conformity. He shows himself on earth as the one who is most silent, most despoiled, and most pliant before the Father's designs, yet at the same time as the one who is most alive, most energetic, and most distinctive in the entire history of mankind.

How can that be? Through filial love. Jesus doesn't sacrifice his plan, he realizes it in God's plan. He doesn't abandon his will, he accomplishes it in God's will. Free because he is a Son, he shares his liberty (see John 8:36) with whoever receives from him "the Spirit of adoption as sons, by whom we cry, 'Abba! Father!' " (Romans 8:15).

The Way of the Cross

But in order to be conformed to order and liberty, what I ask of you will still cost you self-will, self-glory, self-reliance, self-righteousness—the whole natural man. Yes, it costs, and perhaps more than you and I think, unless we have seriously attempted this unreserved renunciation. This is the great sacrifice. This is the crucifixion of the Christian life.

Very well, this crucifixion is learned from Jesus Christ crucified. Place yourself in front of that cross on which he suffered all and accomplished all in order to conform himself to the Father's will, and there will no longer be anything in the divine plans that you refuse to accomplish or to suffer. If the cross of Jesus Christ hasn't taught you that, it hasn't taught you anything. If there is even a spark of Christian faith and Christian life in you, your heart, far from resisting the doctrine of my text, will go out to meet it with a holy jealousy.

Then the carrying out of the divine plan will be for you not just an obligation but a privilege; not just a privilege, but a need. It will be your hunger and your thirst. Henceforth you will substitute lively agreement for the cold admiration you have perhaps thus far granted to your Savior's statement, "My food is to do the will of him who sent me and to accomplish his work" (John 4:34).[9]

PRAYER

God of Jeremiah, God of Jesus Christ, we have known that "it is not in man who walks to direct his steps" (Jeremiah 10:23), and we come to you to place the direction of our steps into your fatherly hands! "Correct [us], O LORD, but in justice; not in your anger, lest you bring [us] to nothing" (Jeremiah 10:24). May a streak of lightening split the sky, even in the midst of our darkness, in order to reveal your plan and your designs to us, so that henceforth we may unreservedly desire to enter into them! Put an end to our infinite perplexities, to our perpetual groping, to our society without principles, to our Church without a common life, and to our Christianity without a Christian life!

Beyond that, Lord, may you yourself speak in place of the one who speaks! He, too, has known that man's words do not depend on him, and that it is not in man who speaks to direct his discourses (Proverbs 16:1). He waits for you alone to guide this people and to guide him into the paths where you deign to be found!

---

[9] At this point a section has been omitted. It begins with the words, "I would be finished, if I were speaking elsewhere or at a different time," and goes on to address the political and religious upheaval peculiar to the France of his day.

7

THE HAPPINESS OF THE CHRISTIAN LIFE

☙

(Montauban)

O LORD of hosts, blessed is the one who trusts in you! — Psalm 84:12[1]

CONCEPTIONS OF THE CHRISTIAN LIFE

You have often heard it proclaimed that "Christ died for our sins in accordance with the Scriptures" (1 Corinthians 15:3). Others have joined with John the Baptist to tell you, "Whoever believes in the Son has eternal life; whoever does not obey the Son shall not see life, but the wrath of God remains on him" (John 3:36). You have been forcefully admonished to flee the coming wrath, to believe, to be converted. How is it that these words leave you cold and that most of you seem to take no heed of these solemn warnings? I am convinced that it's not because you have formed the dreadful plan of rejecting God's grace and throwing yourselves in desperation into eternal perdition. No, the goal

---

[1] The French word for "blessed" in this verse can also be translated "happy".

that is offered to you seems desirable enough; you just don't like the path that takes you there. Whatever the hopes of the Christian faith might be, the Christian life frightens you. It is, in your opinion, a life devoid of charm and interest, filled with hardship and sacrifice.

Even if the Christian life were as sad as you paint it, the knowledge that it is the only means of arriving at the blessed life should be sufficient for you, for it would be folly—even you will agree—to balance transitory suffering against eternal bliss. But in the end, there is nothing more false than your conception of the Christian life. If you were familiar with it, you would know that, on the contrary, it is the happiest of lives, the only happy life, even down here. You would know that "godliness . . . holds promise for the present life and also for the life to come" (1 Timothy 4:8). That is what the Holy Spirit declares in the words of my text and what I propose to demonstrate to you today.

The Nature of the Promised Happiness

But even as I celebrate the happiness of the Christian life, I fear that you might counter with an argument based on experience. "If the Christian life is so happy, why aren't true Christians more content? Why do some of them even seem sad and preoccupied much of the time?" This difficulty has to do with you, children of God, who are part of this assembly.

Where is the Joy?

If I were only interested in justifying you, I would not be totally at a loss for answers. I could point out to those who speak that way that, on the whole, there is much more contentment and peace among the true disciples of Jesus Christ than among others. I could point out to them that the happiness of the Christian life is a serious happiness, which is shown less on the outside than it is felt on the inside.

I could point out to them that we are surrounded down here with scenes of sin and unbelief, and, alas, still carry their stubborn remnants around with us. It is therefore no wonder that we sometimes bend under the weight of human misery.

I could also point out to them that it is only fair to make allowance among some for a disposition of character or even a physical state that predisposes them to gloominess and which, before their conversion, pushed them to despair.

I could tell you all that, my dear listeners, but I doubt that these explanations would fully satisfy you because they don't fully satisfy me. There is a treasure of joy and power in the Christian faith that should suffice for our greatest needs. Beyond that, I have not climbed into this pulpit to preach Christians, but to preach Christ. That's why I would rather simply confess before God and man that for the most part we lack joy because we are people of little faith.

An Inner Joy

Whatever our situation and personal experience, it remains true that joy is a fruit of the Spirit (Galatians 5:22) and that there is nothing impractical about God commanding his children to "Rejoice always" (1 Thessalonians 5:16). This is a point on which I will have no difficulty convincing you, if you will listen to me with an open mind. As for those of us who have believed, may this discourse give us a better sense of the grandeur of our privileges so that we may become happier and, in the process, better suited to glorify the Lord!

The happiness that we promise you in the Christian life is not—does it need to be said?—an outward, earthly, carnal contentment such as the world can give. That is a transitory bliss, incapable of satisfying the human heart, and those who content themselves with it don't even have the sad consolation of being able to carry it with them into hell. No, I speak of an inner, spiritual, heavenly bliss; one suited to a man who senses the dignity of his nature and the enormous needs of his heart. Therefore, lift your spirits up above your ordinary attachments and enter into more noble thoughts.

One aspect of the happiness of the Christian life is so striking that it must surely dazzle every eye. It is the aspect that David celebrates at the opening of Psalm 32: "Blessed is the one whose transgression is forgiven, whose sin is covered." The assurance of having received forgiveness for our sins is the first grace that God gives to a sinner, but it is never alone. Along with it, we receive all the other gifts set forth in the remainder of this beautiful psalm: consolation in life's troubles and God's light in its darkness while awaiting a peaceful death and a blessed eternity. Receiving these things is not just one of the joys of a Christian; it is *the* joy. It is a joy such as you who do not have the happiness of believing cannot sometimes help sighing after. But that, too, is not what I came to talk to you about.

A Paradoxical Joy

I want to suppose that you are fully persuaded of all that, and I prefer to use this discourse to show you truths of which you have not the slightest idea and that will, at first glance, seem to you like strange paradoxes. I want to make you desire the Christian life not through its more glorious side but through its more solemn sides. I want to make you see that the very characteristics that most repel you in this life actually conceal secret charms beneath misleading appearances. I want you to know that just as "the foolishness of God is wiser than men, and the weakness of God is stronger than men" (1 Corinthians 1:25), so the bitterness of the life he sends to his children is sweeter than all the sweetness of this world's life.

The Happiness of Believing

In effect, what is it that you dislike about the Christian life? First of all, it is faith; it is that submissive spirit that Jesus Christ requires of those who belong to him. You see this submission as tied to credulity, and that alone is enough to keep you from agreeing to it. Your intellect needs to be satisfied or you can know no happiness. We agree with you that happiness is impossible if our intellect isn't satisfied, but far from requiring blind credulity, faith is the best use we can make of our reason, gaining for us an intellectual happiness we have found nowhere else.

A Question of Authority

A submissive spirit is not always credulity. Someone is only credulous in submitting himself to an authority that doesn't deserve the confidence he places in it. For example, a child who orders his life based on the pronouncements of another child just as inexperienced as he, or a child who believes every old wives' tale with which a foolish maid servant fills his ears is, no doubt, being credulous. But does this term really describe a child who, recognizing that he is incapable of looking after himself, relies on his father's direction? Isn't he acting with more sense than if he prided himself on his independence and wanted to follow only his own counsel? May this analogy instruct you.

We Christians believe that we, too, are making excellent use of our intelligence in recognizing that we are far more ignorant and dependent before God than this child is before his father. We thus resolve to submit ourselves to the Bible, which, in our eyes, is the Word of God.

Perhaps you are saying under your breath, "That's fine if we were assured that the Bible really is God's Word, but how do you know that? Can that itself be accepted without credulity?" Ah, if you think you have to close your eyes in order to accept the marks of divinity in the Bible, think again! Whoever seeks in all simplicity to know whether the Bible is of God will be irresistibly convinced, and whoever has already received it as God's Word finds abundant proof that he has judged correctly. He finds it not only in those miracles and prophesies that are as well attested as the most authentic histories of ages past; not only in that inner voice through which the Holy Spirit testifies to him that he has judged correctly. He sees it written everywhere—in heaven, on earth, and in the heart and life of man.

Solving the World's Enigmas

The world is full of enigmas that the Bible, and the Bible alone, can explain. Bring us your philosophical doctrine and gather together all your wise men. As for me, I will bring you the simplest among my brothers—the peasants, the children—but with the Bible in their hands.

Explain sin to us; explain how, under the government of a holy God, the thought of the first disobedience entered into the heart of the first man. We, in turn, will explain it to you through the simple story of the tree of the knowledge of good and evil. Perhaps this account has more than once excited your derision, yet it holds more light on this most obscure question than there is in all of your philosophies put together.

Explain death to us; explain how this fearful disorder was born under the government of a good and wise God. What am I saying, death? Explain sickness to us; explain suffering, explain the smallest pain, explain a little scratch. We, in turn, will explain every suffering, large and small, along with death, which exceeds them all, through this statement from the book we hold in our hands: "Sin came into the world through one man, and death through sin" (Romans 5:12).

Explain history to us; explain what divine plan can be untangled from the dreadful confusion of crimes that stain our race and of calamities that desolate it. We, in turn, will explain it through those prophesies that show centuries ahead of time four great empires rising one after another, falling one on top of another, and finally giving way to a kingdom that shall have no end.

What more shall I say? The Bible clarifies all the great problems of humanity which, from age to age, have caused the despair of philosophy. Doubtless, it doesn't clarify them in a way that leaves no questions to be asked, but it clarifies them in a way that justifies God and satisfies man. By the light that it begins to shed today, it gives us a foretaste of a still brighter light that will dispel all our darkness.

It is through this testimony of fact and experience that we are assured, with evidence that only grows from day to day, that the Bible is surely what it claims to be: God's book.

Satisfying Our Intellects

After all of that, how can you tell us that we are credulous for submitting to the Bible? Ah, we would be truly credulous if we could believe that such a book was produced by man's hand or if, knowing that it came from God, we could submit to some other authority. But now we rejoice, we glory in being submitted to it, since this is the best use we can make of our reason. The intellectual happiness of which the world falsely boasts, we truly find in faith.

It is with good conscience, it is without in any way infringing on the rights of human reason, it is in the full enjoyment of all our soul's faculties that we can savor the happiness of believing.

Yes, the happiness of believing! Words fail us to bless God for the fact that, amidst the opposing views clashing and battling all around us, we have a word from God, a written word, that reveals to poor sinners the way to eternal life, "Jesus Christ and him crucified" (1 Corinthians 2:2).

Yes, the happiness of believing! While everyone else is consumed by their vain search for someplace to settle their wandering thoughts and can arrive only at conjectures in place of the conviction they yearn for, we know a deep peace.

Yes, the happiness of believing! The happiness of being able to say, not only before men but even before God and in our secret thoughts, "The grace in which we are established is the true grace!" Our assurance is called a crime, and we are told to present our conviction only as a debatable opinion. Yet that's impossible. Let doubt speak the language of doubt; faith says, "Thus saith the Lord."

Lord, we bear witness of you before men; may you too bear witness of us in the hearts of our listeners until that great day when every eye shall see you coming on the clouds of heaven! "O LORD of hosts, blessed is the one who trusts in you!"

THE HAPPINESS OF A UNIFIED FOCUS

What else do you dislike about the Christian life? It seems to you to be monotonous or, to put it bluntly, tedious. You see it as going round and round in the narrow circle of two or three ideas—read the Bible and pray, pray and read the Bible—an existence as unvarying as it is cold, and one to which a lively spirit could not submit. You will, perhaps, find us to be quite audacious if we dare to assert that, on the contrary, the Christian life has more action and interest than yours.

UNITY, NOT UNIFORMITY

First of all, what you take for uniformity is, in fact, unity. We willingly grant you that a Christian's entire life is summed up (or at least should be), not in two or three thoughts, but in only one: Jesus Christ. For the Christian, "to live is Christ" (Philippians 1:21). Believing in Jesus Christ, loving Jesus Christ, serving Jesus Christ, imitating Jesus Christ—that is the "one thing . . . necessary" (Luke 10:42). But you don't really understand human nature if you think that the Christian life will have less interest because it is completely focused on a single goal.

As all philosophers have observed, it is the nature of our spirit to seek a unique design, a unifying principle in everything, so that we cannot be content where we fail to find unity.

If your life does not have a primary interest that completely dominates it, like a center around which it moves; if you propose one goal for yourself one day and a different goal the next day; if you sometimes seek direction from what the world approves, sometimes from the example of others, sometimes from the inclination of your heart, and sometimes from God's commandment, then your life will lack unity. It will be without power, without depth, and without purpose. Or rather, it won't even be a life worthy of the name, but only a series of events.

Ah, be assured that we would have to lose both our sense of human dignity and our sense of Christian duty before we could agree thus to dissipate a spirit that God made in his image. Be assured that, if we had to make the choice, we would rather have unity without variety—an unvarying life like that of recluses—than variety without unity, which only leads to the kind formless life you boast of.

But this choice is unnecessary; the Christian life brings everything together. Under that powerful unity of a focus on Jesus Christ is arrayed an infinite variety of goals which we can undertake in the name of the Lord. And what beside sinning cannot be done to his glory? The work of six days and the rest of the seventh, fatigue and relaxation, the obligations and honors of civic life, the duties and sweetness of domestic life, the training of soul, spirit, and body, and even the eating of food that the Christian sanctifies through prayer—all that can be related to the Lord. And we can fill a day, a week, a year with new and varied concerns without ever ceasing to serve and glorify his name.

That is how the Christian life fulfills, in its way, the best definition that philosophers have ever given of beauty. Beauty, they have said, is unity within variety. Variety and unity—oh, how well these two are joined together in the Christian life. Just as one could not find a more beautiful sight in the physical realm than the firmament strewn with stars, whose infinite motions obey one and the same law, so too one could not find a lovelier sight in the moral realm than the Christian life, where one single thought permeates and dominates all the useful concerns of human existence.

The Example of Family Life

Perhaps these reflections are a bit abstract and hard for some of you to grasp. Let's clarify them with an example taken from family life. In a house where the Lord Jesus is not loved and served, the relationships between husband and wife, between parents and children, between the head of the house and the servants are only loosely bound and deprived of a common principle. In a Christian household, things are entirely different. An invisible guest lives there, a guest who is seen with the eyes of faith and whose spirit animates all the relationships of family life.

The close and holy relationship between husband and wife finds its basis and pattern in Jesus. You recall that he deigned to call himself the church's bridegroom and to call the church his bride. The husband must love his wife as Christ loved the church (Ephesians 5:25), and the wife must submit to her husband as the church submits to Christ (Ephesians 5:24).

The tender and sweet relationship between parents and their children again finds its basis and pattern in Jesus. God, who has adopted us in him, calls himself our Father and calls us his children. The father must guide his own children as God guides his children in Jesus Christ, and the son must obey his father as a Christian obeys his Father in heaven (Ephesians 6:1-4).

Ordered in this way, family life brings together unity and variety—variety in these diverse relationships and unity in the contemplation of Jesus in whom they are all focused.

Isn't it true that if some sweet cheerfulness, some tender affection, some real joy, some active comfort is found in your home, that it is due to him? Isn't it also true that if there are seasons of dullness or boredom, they are not when he deigns to preside over your interactions; they are not when he is seated with you at the domestic feast, when he breaks the bread that gives life to the soul along with that which nourishes the body, or when he says to you, as he once said to his disciples in the upper room, "Peace be with you" (John 20:19,21,26)?

Your peace, Lord, but along with it the liveliest and deepest interests!

Deep Interests, Not Cold Indifference

Yes, my dear listeners, the liveliest and deepest interests. This astonishes you. We were saying that the Christian life seems uniform to you, but beyond that, it seems cold. There are so many interests and events that draw you and stir you, through hope or anxiety, through joy or sorrow; yet it seems to you that the true Christian remains impassive. He is in a sense isolated, even in the midst of the world, and, according to his own words, a stranger down here, so that the interests of heaven seem to close his heart to those of earth. You cannot envy him this indifference. You need more involvement and more fervor. We, too, need involvement and fervor. Human nature needs it—it is a remnant of our primitive grandeur—but the Christian life, and it alone satisfies this need.

Look deeper, and beneath the agitation of your life you will find interests that are without grandeur or depth, interests unworthy of attracting an immortal soul. On the contrary, beneath the Christian's tranquility you will find only great and deep interests, worthy of his nature and yours. In this regard, one word says it all: your interests are earthly, while his are heavenly. The result is that in you one sees an immortal spirit agitated by the things of time while in him one sees an immortal spirit stirred by the things of eternity.

Eternal, Not Temporal Interests

What, in effect, are those things that fill your life? Shall I speak of your ordinary interests? What? Speak about an evening party, a meal, a suit of clothes, a praise, a criticism? But let's get to your most serious interests. Perhaps it is a matter of knowing whether you will be rich or poor, whether you will lose your health or be able to keep it, whether your life is or is not reaching its end. Very well, what is there in all of that that could fill the immense void of an immortal spirit? For, in the end, rich or poor, you "brought nothing into the world, and [you] cannot take anything out of the world" (1 Timothy 6:7). Sick or healed, your life will end sometime, and if you are saved today, you are going to die tomorrow.

Suppose someone brings you the news that a child has been born into your family, or that someone has died, or that there is a revolution in your country. A newborn child is one more inhabitant on this earth who will bring you several years of joy (or will, perhaps, bring you distress) and will then go off to his rest. A man who has just died is one person less in the world, where the void that he leaves is soon filled. His departure scarcely arouses any interest in you apart from that of the passing affection you had for him. (I am assuming that you are above the miserable preoccupations of an inheritance.) A political upheaval, once the danger is past, is a rearrangement of things or simply of people, and what affects you most is the influence it will have on your personal fortune. All your interests are as short as time, as uncertain as life, as low as the earth.

The Christian's thoughts are completely different. Because he carries Jesus Christ and the Holy Spirit within him, the Christian's heart and eyes have been opened to the invisible and spiritual things. Thus he leaves you to vegetate in time while he alone lives in eternity. His great soul, taught to measure heaven and hell, recognizes within itself the heights of the one and the depths of the other, and he feels the repercussions of all that goes on in the world of the spirits. What he seeks for himself and others is God; it is holiness, it is grace, it is the company of angels, it is eternal life. What he dreads for himself and others is Satan; it is sin, it is cursing, it is the company of demons, it is eternal fire. Am I saved, am I ready to die, am I ripe for the kingdom of heaven?—this is his question for himself and for you.

Binding Earth to Heaven

Do you not sense how this spirit elevates the tiniest details of life by causing them to be seen in the light of eternity? Something that appears insignificant to you is, for him, the subject of serious meditation and fervent prayer, for he does not break his ties with earth, but he binds earth to heaven. The Christian is no less interested than you are in the things of down here. Rather he is more deeply, if more tranquilly interested in them, following the example of God who is "patient because he is eternal."[2]

---

[2] Saint Augustine. [A.M.]

And what shall I say about life's great events? For the Christian, a child who is born is an immortal being who is going to meet an endless happiness or an endless unhappiness. The Lord has confided this child to his care, telling him as Pharaoh's daughter once told Moses' mother, "Take this child away and nurse him for me" (Exodus 2:9).

For him, a man who dies is a soul for whom the time of testing has just ended forever and who, on leaving here, is going to either enjoy heavenly glory or fall into the hands of a God of vengeance. And imagine what goes on in the Christian's heart if this dying person is a friend, a brother, a wife, a father, a child?

For him, a political upheaval is part of the vast plan that God conceived in the beginning and that he unfolds from century to century; a plan to put all nations under the rule of Jesus Christ. All of history is a great drama that must come to this magnificent ending: "the earth shall be full of the knowledge of the LORD as the waters cover the sea" (Isaiah 11:9).

For a Christian, life is so serious, so filled in turn with hopes that transport him to heaven and anguishes that plunge him into the depths that he is sometimes astounded at being able to bear such conflict. He is astounded, yet there is, in the depths of his being, an indefinable something that finds its meaning in these anguishes. He prefers to feel the bitterness of life rather than to escape it through indifference, just as you prefer to feel a heartache rather than to escape it through the unconcern of youth. In the end, in his saddest moments he would not exchange his condition for yours; how much less would he do so in his days of joy, a heavenly joy of which you cannot even conceive!

A Fathomless Sea

After all of that, suppose someone comes to tell us that the Christian life lacks vitality and interest! It must rather be said that these things are found only in the Christian life. There is a vigor and an interest there, beside which all that occupies you has no more importance than your childhood houses of cards have beside your most serious concerns of today.

It is a life of such sweet peace, and at the same time of such deep emotion; a life of such strong unity, and at the same time of such infinite variety; a life, in a word, so alive. It is the only life capable of satisfying a heart that feels and a spirit that thinks. Beside it every other life on earth is only like a corpse next to a man. "O LORD of hosts, blessed is the one who trusts in you!"

The Happiness of Renouncement

Finally, what is it that you dislike about the Christian life? The Christian life is a life of sacrifice and privation; a life of conquering all one's fancies, refusing oneself the most legitimate amusements, living apart. What a sad and unsociable existence, without enjoyment for oneself and equally without usefulness for others! This is where I am waiting for you. What most repels you in the Christian life is what constitutes its charm and its triumph.

Renouncing Self, Not the World

Let there be no confusion as to what we mean by the Christian life. We do not mean withdrawal from the world. Christians, as we use the term, dwell in the world, because they know that that is where God calls them to serve him. As the Lord said, "I do not ask that you take them out of the world" (John 17:15). Christians live in your midst, enjoying the good things of life and fulfilling their duties.

Having explained that, we agree with you that the Christian life is one of renouncement, for it is written, "Any one of you who does not renounce all that he has cannot be my disciple" (Luke 14:33). It is not enough to say that there are sacrifices in the Christian life; the entire Christian life is one great, long sacrifice—the sacrifice of self. After that, all other sacrifices seem small. Man would willingly give up his money, his pleasures, his honor, his rest, his family, his health, and his life rather than renounce himself, his self-will, his self-righteousness, his self-glory.

The Power of a Renewed Will

We grant you all that, but we tell you that though this sacrifice is so bitter to self-will, so impossible to accomplish by ourselves, yet it becomes the source of the highest and purest satisfaction one can taste on this earth for someone with a renewed will. I said for a renewed will, and this is just where I fear to be misunderstood. Yet there is a truth here that resonates so well with the human spirit that you must surely sense something of it. I appeal boldly to you yourselves. Isn't it true that there is a happiness in renouncement and devotion? For there is happiness in loving, and devotion is nothing but love carried to the point where one forgets oneself in favor of the one he loves.

A young girl is completely filled with the world's vanity and pleasures. Sought after, flattered, admired, she is an idol for others and an idol for herself. Then she becomes a wife and mother. At that point, her life changes. Farewell to the pleasures of the world, the pride of adornment, the drunkenness of praises. Day and night, she consecrates herself to her small child. She gazes on him, carries him, caresses him, soothes his cries, nourishes him with her milk. From morning to evening we see her occupied with him, and often, if he cannot sleep, we find her watching over him from evening to morning. Is he sick? She exhausts herself in serving him, and through the care she lavishes on him, she makes herself sicker than he.

I ask you, in replacing those earlier pleasures, without which she felt she could not exist, with this devotion that completely absorbs her today; in ceasing to live for herself and learning to live for another, has she become less happy? Ah, if there is a mother here who recognizes herself in this scene, I am not worried about her answer.

Well then, I turn to her and say: Why do you consider yourself to be happy? How is it that, if someone dared pity you for exchanging your past joy for a life of renouncement, you, in turn, would pity this poor egoist as a man who has never known the heart's true joys? What is it that makes up your happiness, if it is not that we carry within us a heart that hungers and thirsts to love and that finds its complete satisfaction only in giving itself wholly?

Devotion to Christ

How would it be, then, oh tender mother, if, instead of devoting yourself that way to a poor creature—helpless, mortal, sinful—you learned from faith to devote yourself to Jesus, your Creator, your Savior, and your God?[3]

When you devote yourself to your child, you devote yourself to a weak creature who may forever be ignorant of what you have done for him. But when you devote yourself to Jesus, it will be to the mighty God whose hands created heaven and earth and who has promised that "there is no one who has left house or brothers or sisters or mother or father or children or lands, for my sake and for the gospel, who will not receive a hundredfold now in this time, . . . and in the age to come eternal life" (Mark 10:29-30).

---

[3] Here Monod is certainly not belittling a mother's care for her child. His point is that if a child is worthy of whole hearted devotion, how much more is Christ worthy! If devotion to a child brings fulfillment, how much more fulfilling is devotion to Christ! Devotion to Christ should be primary, with devotion to her child flowing out of it.

When you devote yourself to your child, you devote yourself to a fragile creature whom you can serve today and for whom you will perhaps be unable to do anything tomorrow, because you are separated from him either by death or by lands and seas. But when you devote yourself to Jesus, it will be to the one "who lives forever and ever" (Revelation 4:9, 10:6, 15:7) and who fills all things (Ephesians 4:10). Nothing can separate you from him. Finding even a moment of our lives that cannot be spent in serving him is like finding a hollow at the bottom of the sea where the water does not penetrate.

When you devote yourself to your child, you devote yourself to a fallen creature in whom the image of God, which alone can make him loveable, is tarnished by sin. Thus love for him, if it were not governed by God's love, would be out of place and idolatrous. But when you devote yourself to Jesus, it will be to the Holy One.[4] Love for him should have no measure, for he himself serves as the measure of all other love, and it was said of him, "You shall love the Lord your God with all your heart and with all your soul and with all your mind" (Matthew 22:37).

When you devote yourself to your child, you devote yourself to a creature who, having received everything from you and having given you nothing, has a right to your love only through your devotion and your name of mother. But when you devote yourself to Jesus—and it is here above all that I would like to make myself clear—it will be to the one who has first given himself for us. He has given himself completely; given himself on the cross; he the Creator for us his creatures, he the Holy One for us sinners, he the Prince

---

[4] This is literally "the Holy of holies," possibly a reference to the innermost part of the Old Testament tabernacle and later of Solomon's temple. The Holy One is a title often given to Jesus (e.g. Acts 3:14) and expresses Monod's thought here.

of life for us poor slaves of death. Thus he has gained the right to say to us, "You are not your own, for you were bought with a price" (1 Corinthians 6:19-20).

Oh, Jesus. Oh, my God. To devout ourselves to you unreservedly and undividedly; to love you above all else and to love all else only after you and in you and for you—is that then the sadness of the Christian life? Oh, blessed sadness! Lord, make us ever sadder in this way! You who sound the depths of the heart, you know that we are happy to renounce ourselves for you and that what is lacking in our happiness is only to renounce ourselves more fully! Yes, if we could give up everything in order to follow you, if we could love only what you love, do nothing except for your glory, and have no action, no thought, no beat of our hearts that was not for you, then our joy would be complete! Then crosses would be light! Then, while waiting for your heaven—the heaven that your blood has opened for us—we would already have found a heaven on earth in serving you!

Devotion to Those Christ Loves

After all of that, is it needful to add that, just as the sacrifices of the Christian life are not without enjoyment for the Christian himself, so too they are not without usefulness for others? What? Will devotion to Jesus, the Savior of men, not produce devotion to the men whom he has loved so much? If someone is converted to Jesus Christ, you complain that he is lost to society. Lost to society? What a misuse of language! Society would be fortunate if it lost all of us that way! It is because he has become a man of faith and prayer that the true Christian has also become a man of charity and action, an imitator of the one who "went about doing good" (Acts 10:38).

Is it a matter of man's spiritual joy? The Christian alone can help. He alone works at this admirable task whose object is the salvation of the world. He alone acts, prays, and exhorts in order to induce men to turn toward God. Very well, is that not the greatest kindness? Do we truly understand the value of one single immortal soul? What joy, oh, what joy for the one who saves that soul from death!

But when it is a matter of contributing to the temporal joy of our fellow men, perhaps you think that the true Christian will apply himself with less fervor than someone else, accustomed as he is to subordinating temporal things to the eternal. Think again. Here too he will be second to none in zeal and will regularly be seen, according to Saint Paul's lovely phrase, "at the head of good works."[5] It is his own advantages that he has learned to renounce, not the advantages of others. For himself he says, "But none of these things move me, neither count I my life dear unto myself" (Acts 20:24 KJV), but everything moves him when it comes to others. To gain them the slightest relief or spare them the slightest pain is a prize worthy of all his efforts.

The Christian has received this example from his Master, "who . . . endured the cross, despising the shame" (Hebrews 12:2) and who overall spent his life in healing men not only of the sicknesses of the soul, but also of those of the body.

And if the first concern of the Christian is for eternal interests, that will all the more surely guarantee the success of what he does for the interests of the present life, for it is written, "seek first the kingdom of God and his righteousness, and all these things will be added to you" (Matthew 6:33). No, there is no action, there is no devotion, there is no work of charity which may not have its basis and soul in faith, and it is here above all, it is in this life of renouncement and sacrifice that the Christian has occasion to cry out, "O LORD of hosts, blessed is the one who trusts in you!"

---

[5] Literal translation of Titus 3:8 [A.M.]

The Happiness of Having a Savior

And yet, note it well, we have only shown you the happiness of the Christian life by its least obvious aspects. Ask a Christian why he is happy, and he will probably not give you any of the reasons I have just discussed. He will not tell you that the Christian life answers all the needs of his nature, or that it satisfies his intelligence through faith, his soul through passion, or his heart through devotion. Not that all of that doesn't seem true to him or that it doesn't contribute, in effect, to his happiness, but there is something still better than all of that. There is a completely simple answer that comes first to his lips: "I am happy because I have a Savior and my sins have been forgiven."

Do You Know What It's Like?

So far, I have spoken very little about this, because this part of our joy is so obvious and striking that I assumed you would recognize it well enough on your own. But do you really recognize it? Do you know what it is to be able to say, "I am received through grace, my transgression is forgiven, my sins are covered, the Lord does not count my iniquity against me"? (see Psalm 32:1-2). Do you know what it is to have God for your father, Jesus Christ for your brother, the Holy Spirit for your comforter? Do you know what it is to be able to approach God any hour of the day or night with the confidence that he loves us, that he listens to us, that he answers us, that he delivers us, and that he finishes the work of grace he has begun in us?

Do you know what it is to be able to greet all of life's afflictions as a healthy discipline from a Father who loves us and from a Savior who was the first to suffer? Can you greet them as love's testimonies that we would not want to avoid, even if we could, and in which we rejoice, glory, and give thanks? Do you know what it is to have a guide of whom we can seek counsel in the uncertainties that fill our lives; a guide who, having taught the faithful soul to say to him "Teach me to do your will, for you are my God!" (Psalm 143:10), answers him saying "I will instruct you and teach you in the way you should go; I will counsel you with my eye upon you" (Psalm 32:8)?

Do you know what it is to be able to die in peace, seeing the Savior ready to receive us, and saying with the apostle, "I have fought the good fight, I have finished the race, I have kept the faith. Henceforth there is laid up for me the crown of righteousness, which the Lord, the righteous judge, will award to me on that Day" (2 Timothy 4:7-8)?

But above all, do you know what it will be like to enter into possession of that eternal bliss of which all descriptions, even those in the Bible, can give us only an imperfect idea, because they are written in human language? Do you know what it will be like to be admitted to the dwelling place where "death shall be no more, neither shall there be mourning nor crying nor pain anymore" (Revelation 21:4), but where "God [is] all in all" (1 Corinthians 15:28)? Do you know what it will be like to find ourselves reunited with Abraham, Moses, Elijah, and Isaiah; with Saint Paul, Saint Peter, and Timothy; to find ourselves in the company of the holy angels and in the presence of the Lord Jesus, singing the song of the redeemed? "Salvation belongs to our God who sits on the throne, and to the Lamb! . . . Blessing and glory and wisdom and thanksgiving and honor and power and might be to our God forever and ever!" (Revelation 7:10,12). Do you know what that will be like? Do we ourselves know it? "O LORD of hosts, blessed is the one who trusts in you!"

Entering Into the Blessed Life

Oh my brothers, my dear brothers, do you not desire to enter into this path of "godliness" that "is of value in every way, as it holds promise for the present life and also for the life to come" (1 Timothy 4:8)? Would you voluntarily deprive yourselves of eternal life? And why? To be happier in this life? No, but to deprive yourself even down here of the only joy worthy of the name.

When we called you to faith in the name of your salvation, human nature could shrink back before a path that leads to eternal life but that is so rough and so narrow. When we called you there in the name of your sanctification, the flesh could be terrified of such a bitter renunciation of our own will. But when we call you there today in the name of your happiness—of your present happiness as well as your future happiness—oh, who would be foolish enough, who would be his own enemy enough to reject such a great salvation?

And above all, what about you who are afflicted in this world—you who were surrounded by a cherished family and are left alone; you whose ruined health lets you foresee only a life of suffering and a painful death; you who may not lack the necessary things of life, but at least lack all its sweet things? It is you above all others whom God seems to call to peace with Jesus Christ. Would you rather let your tears be lost on the ground than spill them on Jesus' breast?

Is there someone here who is saying within himself, "It's all over! I, too, want to be converted!"? I don't know who you are, oh soul that hungers and thirsts for the peace of Jesus, but God knows you. He sees you in the midst of this assembly, and who but he can arouse those feelings in your heart? Poor blind Bartimaeus, "Take heart. Get up; he is calling you" (Mark 10:49). "Do not fear; only believe" (Luke 8:50). "Have faith and do not doubt" (Matthew 21:21).

The one who is calling you is also the one who will open your eyes. It is Jesus, whose word created heaven and earth; Jesus, who died for you; Jesus, who speaks to your heart; Jesus, who himself asks you as he did that poor blind man, "What do you want me to do for you?" (Mark 10:51). Today, even here, before leaving the place where you are sitting, make a covenant with him. Accept his forgiveness, and give him your heart. Amen.